WTF What the F@&k

A DC Law Enforcement Officer's Perspective, From the Inside Looking Out

WTF What the F@&k

A DC Law Enforcement Officer's Perspective, From the Inside Looking Out

Officer Mac

Officer Mac Books

ISBN 13: 978-0-615-49572-9
LCCN: 2011962086

Printed in the United States of America
Book design by Wendy Arakawa

Table of Contents

Introduction

What I've learned during the past 16 years in law enforcement and the last ten years as a cop in the Metropolitan Washington, DC area is that right is wrong and wrong is right; good is bad and bad is good. Everything is actually its opposite. That being said, the people reading this book are going to believe or not believe the inner workings of this agency. They will believe or not believe the things that are written in this book. I know that officers from major departments for the most part will believe the stories, and the officers from the particular agency referred to in this book will believe what they are reading because they experience it on a daily basis.

I was once asked to compare this job to another. I really couldn't come up with a reasonable response. It took some searching, but I came up with an answer. The closest job I could think of was an animal control officer. If you are a police officer, I'm sure you can see the correlation. This is, of course, what I do. I track down and capture wild animals, place them in cars with cages, and take them to another place that has bigger cages. Sometimes their owners come get them, sometimes they don't. Many times the animals just sit in a cage for several days, months, and/or years. At times, we are forced to shoot the animals and put them out of their misery. Sometimes the animals are put to sleep. Many times the animals are set free and are returned to their natural habitat.

You might think I'm twisted or crazy, but guess what? That's the way of the world. Therefore, I must maintain a certain mindset in order to function in this kind of environment. Many of you won't immediately comprehend what I'm talking about, but you cops will. This is not a put down of anyone, but many will be offended. If you are, too bad. Trust me, you will get over it. This is from the perspective of a police officer who has vast experience dealing with the public and the antics they engage in. Remember, I'm on the inside looking out, not the outside looking in.

This area of Metropolitan Washington, DC—also known as the DMV, the District, Maryland, and Virginia—is an area all to itself. The people are so different from anywhere else I have visited. This is just a glimpse of the DMV and a particular law enforcement agency. These are the experiences and stories of Officer Mac.

Welcome to my world.

Chapter One

Niggaz vs. Black Folks

First of all, I want white people to know there is a difference between niggaz and black folks. I know many white people like to lump all black people into the same category, but this is a grave mistake. Someone once asked me how you know someone is a nigga. I said, "It's like pornography; I know it when I see it."

What is a nigga? A nigga is someone who does not want to excel—the one who drops out of high school to hang with his boys, sells drugs, lives up under his mother, and eats fried chicken on the corner, throwing the bones in the street; the one who has four babies' mothers and 10 children by them. He won't take care of his children, and is in and out of jail, obtained HIV while in prison and passes it on to other black women, can't read or write, robs, steals, and kills others in his community (hood) because he actually thinks it is his hood. A nigga believes the neighborhood belongs to him, is ignorant, uneducated, wears his pants off of his ass, and rides around on rims; his car pay payment is more than his rent, and he lives in section eight housing and can't pay the rent.

The creation and evolution of niggaz, how did they come to be? Let's see, in the '60s the government made stipulations about having the black male in the residence (low-income housing) if the couple living there had children. The bottom line was the black male was no longer to stay in the same household as the woman and child. For each child the black woman had, she would receive more money. Now how can the male—who is supposed to be the head of the household—be in charge when he can't stay there? The government has groomed these children to be dependent on their mothers. The girls will be somewhat strong like their mothers, and the boys will be physically strong but mentally weak and dependent upon their mothers. So when the children grow up, the males are seeking the mother figure who took care of them when they were children. They have become psychologically dependent on that woman. The male doesn't know anything else.

That void of having a strong male in the household is devastating. Keep in mind, this was done by design. As any intelligent person knows, the family is the nucleus. Without both parental figures in the household, the family structure weakens. If one wants to make a group weaker, the first thing to do is break down the family. If you want to create a sub-group of a group to commit crimes and become incarcerated, lack morals and values, be buffoons and act stupid, lack critical thinking skills, and not be able to think rationally, start using drugs and alcohol, and add mindless entertainment this is the way to do it, because one woman taking care of many children is not going to be able to accomplish this on her own.

This is the beginning of the destruction of blacks and the creation of niggaz . As the cycle perpetuates, this is what you get. This has taken place over the last 40 years and the full effect of the niggaz is here.

The nigga is a weak individual, mentally, because he has not had a sufficient environment in which to grow and mature. Physically he is strong, he can intimidate, instill fear, and is violent; but he is uneducated and ignorant. He doesn't even know that he is a nigga because of the environment in which he lives. He is surrounded by other niggaz. Therefore, he thinks this is "the norm." The nigga is a detriment to society and needs to be eradicated. Niggaz cause so much damage and destruction to blacks (not so much whites) that they need to be stopped. I know most people think this is harsh or cruel, but this is reality.

I will provide real examples of what niggaz do based upon my experiences. My partner and I responded for a family disturbance call. Upon arrival, there was a male and female. The female said, "I want that motherfucker out of the house!" We wanted to know why. She said, "He's an asshole." We asked the male, "What's going on?" The male was in the bedroom. He told us that she was angry because he smoked the last of the crack. We went back into the living room where the female was and asked her if this was true. She said, "Yeah, it's true." I asked, "Why would you call the police for this?" She became angry and said,

"You, you redd nigga you." She called me "redd nigga" because of my complexion. "Who do you think you are?" My partner said, "Mac, don't even engage her. That's the crack talking." My partner and I just looked at one and other left the scene.

We always received calls for "a man with a gun." This was a common call because we served a high crime area, specifically for guns, drugs, shootings, stabbings and domestic violence assaults, robberies, and homicides. There were four hucks (huck is short for a person who hangs on the street all day, smoking, drinking, and disturbing the peace) in the alley when we approached by vehicle. When they spotted us, they quickly walked away. Now, I told the officer I was training to take two of them, and I'd take the other two.

Once we had all four stopped, they placed their hands on the vehicle and were told not to move. I attempted to conduct a pat-down for officer safety. One of the hucks kept moving his hand from the cruiser. I told him three times, "Keep your hand on the car." Three times is too many when telling someone to do something. He attempted to move again. This time, I slammed him on his neck. Once I used force (also known as "act right") on this huck, the other three hucks became overly compliant. They didn't even think about moving. You know why? Niggazs understand force. Listen, you can't be nice to niggaz.

I observed a vehicle traveling without its headlights running; of course I was traveling in the opposite direction. I turned around and caught up with the vehicle, turned on my emergency equipment, and attempted to pull him over. He pulled over, and before I could get out of my seatbelt, he was already out of the car without a coat. Now this had to have been the coldest night in DC that year by far. I had on thermals, a turtleneck, and a sweater, and this guy was out without a coat. The first thing he said was, "I didn't do anything." By then, another officer was with me. We handcuffed this huck, placed him in my cruiser, and I ran a check on his driver's license to determine whether or not he had a criminal status. Of course, he was wanted for a traffic warrant. Not only that, but he was wanted on a criminal warrant for assault with a deadly weapon. Furthermore, this huck had committed a homicide and was out on parole.

After we searched the car, we found a 44 magnum is his coat and numerous individually wrapped pieces of crack cocaine. That's called "possession with the intent to distribute while armed." I had removed this huck from the street for a very long time. This happened to be a United States District Court case. Bottom line, if he had gotten out of his car with that gun, I wouldn't be here telling my stories right now.

I was working a high drug trafficking area in Northeast DC. The traffickers were selling PCP. Actually, this drug gang was responsible for numerous homicides and shootings in the area. This was the largest PCP operation in the United States at the time, and most of the money was made in the DMV. I responded to shootings or homicide scenes at least three days a week, where the victim or victims had holes in their head, or multiple bullet holes in his chest. As cops, our job was to disrupt the organization. We conducted a contact on many individuals from outside the area. From the contact, it led to a stop, then an arrest from them buying or possessing PCP.

A federal agency had a RICO (**Racketeer Influenced and Corrupt Organizations Act)** case against this gang. I remember a source of mine called me late at night. He said, "Mac, I have some information for you. The gang put out a hit on an officer." The perpetrators said they were going to place a fake call to the location and when the officer stepped out of the vehicle, they were going to shoot and kill him.

Once I received this information, I called the district, passed the information on, and the officer was removed from that area of town. After the investigation was over, these gang members were given the death penalty and/or given life sentences without the possibility of parole. Here is the bottom line of this story: these niggaz were so ruthless that they were going to kill a cop just for doing his job. This officer disrupted their flow of money and was kicking their ass, so they had planned to kill him.

I have responded to numerous radio runs for a missing person or juvenile. Now listen, no black kids from the city go missing. First of all, their parents don't want them. Therefore, what makes you think someone would actually take them? This is code for: "Their parents don't know where they are and want the police to go pick them up, because niggaz are too lazy to do so." How is it that you as a parent don't know where your children hang out? You don't know who your children's friends are. I know many of you are saying, "Yeah, this is true." Well guess what? I'm talking about you, Niggaz. Take care of your kids, know who their friends are, know where they hang out, and know phone numbers of their friends so you can search for them without having to call the police. Furthermore, there are two ways for niglets (baby niggaz) to go missing:

1) if the mother kills them; or
2) if someone takes the kids to settle a drug debt.

Other than that, those niglets don't go missing.

Why do niggaz call the police for family disturbances? Listen, you are adults; solve your own problems. Stop calling the police. What am I going to do because you had an argument? Just as long as there is not any violence, don't call. You are children. As a stated earlier, niggaz have not developed mentally. Therefore, they still have the mentality of children. So when they call the police, (Daddy and Mommy) we have to be the parents and tell them to stop and go to their rooms. Grow up, niggaz.

Why do niggaz wear their pants off of their ass? You know, you niggaz think that's cool. Well it isn't. Pull your pants up; you look like fucking retards. Every time I see you with your pants off of your ass, I want to give you a wedgie, pull your underwear up over your head, and send you on your way.

My partner and I were working in a certain area that is a so-called "hot spot." We saw a group of hucks on the block and told them to move along. My partner noticed one of them leaning on someone's car. My partner asked if it was his car. He said, "No," and left. About an hour later, we returned and saw the same huck was on a different car. My partner asked him if that was his car. He stated, "No," again. So my partner Id'd the huck. I asked if he ever owned anything in his life. He gave no response. I told him that was the problem. "Because you don't own anything, you don't respect someone else's property. When you get your own things and someone destroys them, then you will know how it feels." I asked him, "Do you own a car?" He said he did but that he was in an accident. He said he was drinking and driving and wrecked it. I asked him, "What have you been locked up for in the past?" Of course he said for drug dealing. I asked him, "With all the money you made from dealing drugs, what did you do with it?" He gave no response. I then asked him, "Do you have a job?" He said, "Yes." He worked at a daycare center. I said, "You mean people actually let you watch their children?" He said, "Yeah." I then asked, "Are you serious? What person in his right mind would let you watch his children?" Now this huck was about 20 years old, 5'7", slender, twists in his hair, and a do-rag on top of his head—a convicted felon. All I could say was, "Wow."

A bicycle officer who was in my academy class, and another officer, were intentionally struck by a juvenile nigga in a stolen vehicle.

The bicycle officer was on patrol and had stopped in an alley. The juvenile decided that because he didn't like police officers, he was going to run them down. The little nigga accomplished his goal. This animal floored the gas pedal and struck the officer, knocking him up over the car. The officer sustained serious bodily injuries. The officer had several surgeries to repair his face from all of the damage caused by this nigga. Thank God this animal was caught and is now incarcerated. When talking to the officer after the assault with the intent to kill (AWIK) he said to me, "Mac, there is only one justice—street justice." I hope you can understand the animosity an officer can acquire after a near life-ending experience.

One thing I noticed after being on numerous homicide scenes was, for the most part, there were chicken bones no more than 10 to 15 feet from the scenes. Now, I'm not psychic, but I knew some niggaz had to be involved. One reason was the obvious: the homicides were in the hood. But the other was simply the fact that they were chicken bones. Like I said regarding the definition of niggaz, they will throw the chicken bones in the street.

As I stated earlier, I see the destruction that niggaz cause—the shootings, beatings, robberies, homicides, and drug-related homicides during which they torture their victims before killing them. It's funny how niggaz get mad at the police when we have to shoot one of these wild animals. But no one complains when they kill each other. You know why I don't care that they kill each other? Because that is one less nigga I have to deal with. I know what you're thinking. *What the fuck? Calling them animals.*

Well, I call a spade a spade. There is no excuse for this type of behavior. I don't understand how anyone can condone this type of behavior. I really see no hope for these people. Well, I really can't call them people. The only remedy I see is the eradication of this group. They are a non-productive group in society.

The evolution of niggaz is complete. It's rather hard to eradicate these animals; Furthermore, they breed like roaches. As I said, niggaz were created by design and, as you can see, this is the end result.

Many times I have been involved in a foot or car pursuit with niggaz. I always felt like I'm on a safari chasing wild animals. Not only that, but they are in their natural habitat. We have the helicopter in the air flying overhead, with the area lit up; all I need then is a net. Sometimes it takes several officers to apprehend niggaz when they are on the run and are evading capture. They needed to change my call sign from 5904 to Animal Control 2.

Let's discuss black people. There are many black people who are good people. They, for the most part, have family values, they get up and go to work every day, and they go to school to obtain an education. Black people do things for the betterment of themselves and their families, just as other races do. I can't say anything bad about black people, because they try to do what is right. Black people won't put a gun to the back of your head and say, "Come up off them pockets, you know what time it is?" or, "Gimme your shit." You don't have to worry about black people breaking into your house. You can go out with black people, and don't have to worry about getting shot or something violent happening to you. For the most part, no matter what your skin color, we all have the same values. Black people will make sacrifices for their children in order for them to have a better future. They understand what hard work is. They understand the value of life. They take care of their children. Black people understand what it is like to have somethingof value and to take care of it. They won't destroy it within a matter of months.

I have nothing but respect for black people. With that being said, I'm seeing the brainwashing take effect on the black community. Are they starting to embrace niggaz? I hope not. Remember, black people keep them separate. They are not like us. We are not like them. Even though we may look alike, we don't talk the same, we don't dress the same. We sure as hell don't act the same. Sometimes we eat at the same restaurants and attend the same sporting events.

Black people: Don't let the niggaz infiltrate our inner circles. Don't let them date your daughters and get them pregnant. Don't let your sons date the women and get them pregnant. If so, those children will take on the traits of the nigga. You will have some serious problems. They will be destructive; they won't know how to act in public. You will be shamed as a family. Furthermore, there is a financial responsibility that goes along with this. The nigga male is not going to support the baby. Now you, as a grandparent, will have to help out. I know grandparents like to help out, but when dealing with niglets (baby niggaz), it's something different. It's a totally different concept. Keep in mind, niggaz are a government creation.

I say this with the utmost sincerity. I want all black parents to make sure your children get a good education. Make sure they attend universities and then graduate school. I cannot emphasize this enough. This specifically goes to the black males. Your education is priority number one. Also, don't get introduced into the criminal justice system, as a young black male. That's what the niggaz are for. These niggaz keep me employed.

I remember I was sitting in DC Superior Court with another black officer from my agency. We were looking at all of the niggaz coming into the courthouse. They were, of course, defendants. Their pants were hanging off of their asses. They even brought their niglets to court with them. Three or four of them dressed like garbage. Their girlfriends had blue, red, and green hair, just looking a mess. This officer said to me, "Mac, Hitler had the right idea, just the wrong group of people."

Chapter Two
Dumbass Whitey

Now I'm going to talk about white people and their actions, and how they think they are superior to everyone else. In all actuality, most of them are idiots. This is not true of all white people, just the majority. Since I've been working in the Capitol Hill area for some time, I've gotten to see more white people and deal with them. I know they think they are above the law, and that the law doesn't apply to them. They whine, bitch, and moan. They are big babies. I'll tell you a few stories of how I know. This, of course, is coming from firsthand experience.

I was called to a house for a burglary report. When I arrived, the complainant was in the middle of the street waving me down. Look, believe me, we can see you. Even before I could get out of my cruiser, she started bombarding me with, "Are you going to help me? I was burglarized; do you care?" Honestly, I don't care, and I really don't want to help you. Of course, I'm saying this in my mind. The reality is, I was pleasant and kept a professional demeanor about myself and said, "I care," and I was there for her. As I went to observe for signs of forced entry, she told me that she was out of town for a week and the newspapers were left in front of the house. She also advised me that she never put the blinds down. Now, everyone knows (except white people) when you're going on vacation, you have the papers stop being delivered. Also, put your blinds or curtains down. Most white people in DC think they are back in Kansas or Podunk or wherever they came from. Better yet, Swamp Water somewhere. Keep in mind, you are in the inner city. The city didn't come to you; you came to it. So just learn to adjust. If you can't, leave.

You leave your purses, laptop computers, and other valuables in your car expecting them to be there when you return to your vehicles. Nine chances out of ten, they won't be. Our crime rate increases all the time because of dumb white people like you. You think because you're on Capitol Hill or you have money, that's going to protect you. It doesn't. That's a false sense of security.

Many times we see white women walking down the street at night, sometimes by themselves. A lot of times we make bets before a call comes out, saying, "What time do you think she'll get robbed?" That's because we know who are targets of criminals. We might even give you a heads-up saying, "Be careful, take off the headsets," or, "Put down the cell phone and pay attention." And of course, we get the response of, "I know what I'm doing. You don't have to tell me." Our response is, "Okay." Later on that night, rest assured we will get a call for a robbery force and violence, or an armed robbery. When we get there on the scene, they are always crying, saying, "I don't know what happened. He took my purse, Ipod, or cell phone."

I just get on the scene and say nothing. What I really want to say is, "Dummy, I just told you two hours ago to be careful."

Why is it that white people always get hit by cars? You know that's why we have crosswalks. You know the two parallel white lines that you walk in between from sidewalk to sidewalk. There are also crossing signals. Why do white people like to cross when the hand is red? Okay, listen idiots that means don't cross. When the light turns white and you see the signal for walking, then you cross. Now, it really doesn't bother me when you get hit by a bus, truck, or car. You know why? Because if you're stupid enough to cross or step out on the street when the hand is red, you deserve to get hit. Not only that, you are only a report. Dispatchers give me numbers for a 10-50 pedestrian with injuries. For those of you who don't know, a 10-50 is a motor vehicle accident.

Why do white people bring their pets to restaurants to eat with them? Look, this is taking it a bit too far, don't you think? As I walk or ride around, I see white people with their dogs sitting outside of a restaurant. Their dogs eating with them, dogs sitting underneath the tables, sitting on people's laps. White people even bring their dog bowls with them for the dogs. I even saw this white girl bring her pet rabbit with her. I said, "Oh, shit, a rabbit on a leash." Now keep in mind, I know the difference between a service animal and a pet. These are pets. I don't think they have service rabbits. What are you whiteys thinking about? Let me guess, dogs are like your children. Well, here's some advice, leave your children at home. They will be okay by themselves for a little while. Okay, whitey? Get a clue.

White people buying drugs in black neighborhoods or areas, understand this: when we see a white person walking into a high drug trafficking area, perhaps in an area with niggaz, we already know what you are there for. Therefore, your activity is deemed to be suspicious. Guess what? I can stop and interview you. Ask you anything about your activity in the area. What I really want to know is where and from whom did you buy the crack or heroin. You are like a fish out of water. Remember the Sesame Street song: *One of These Things Doesn't Belong*? Well guess what? That would be you.

Okay, now you're stopped. I'm going to ask you several questions, like, "Who did you visit?" I get answers like, "A friend, I know people inside." My next question is, "Where do they live?" I guess that's a tricky question, because I can't get a response. My next stumper is, "What is this person's name?" This is how dumb whitey is. Don't you know he has the audacity to say a name like Pookie. "I went to visit Pookie." Of course, I play along. I say I know Pookie. Then I say, "Let's go back and talk to Pookie." It's almost like he is about to shit his pants. His next lie is, "He left." Okay. I ask, "Do you have a phone number for him?" He always replies with, "No." Now, where are the drugs? They give up the drugs and they go to jail. It's that simple.

Listen, whitey, stay out of an area in which you don't belong. Actually, I like to see white people destroy their lives with heroin and other drugs. Not only that, I would hate to get a call of a robbery, when in fact it's just some white guy or girl trying to buy drugs and get ripped off. That would be a "no report." I'm 10-8, dispatcher. (10-8 is a code used to say we are back in service.)

The winter of 2010 was a rough one. We had two blizzards back-to-back, which paralyzed the DMV. Pretty much no one was supposed to be out driving around, and it was a good idea to keep off of the streets. The city was shut down. Take a guess who was outside. Whitey. They were out walking in the center of the streets, had their skis out, skiing around the DMV, walking their dogs in the middle of the street. I'm trying to get to work and when you hit your horn to alert them, don't you know they have the audacity to get an attitude because I'm trying to pass. My question is, why you are walking around in the middle of the street? Where do you have to go? Nothing is open; what are you doing? These people are nuts. What a bunch of weirdoes. This is their logic: I'm going to walk around because I can.

This is another example of how dumb white people are. When we are working a suspicious package, and we have the yellow police tape around a large area, the tape says: police line, don't cross. Why do white people ask if they can cross? They ask me all the time, "Can I cross?" I ask them, "Can you read the fine black print on the yellow tape?" Then they ask what's going on. You tell them. Most white people are like, *A suspicious package here in Washington, DC?* My response is, "Yes, sir or ma'am." But what I really want to say is, "Yeah, you dumbass, where do you think you are?" Keep in mind, this is the terrorists' second target to hit next to New York City. But the funniest thing to do to white people is when they start asking a whole bunch of questions about a suspicious package. I say, "See those SUV's over there? That's the bomb squad." Those whiteys say, "Oh my," then haul ass, and they don't bother you anymore.

I received a call for a tree down in the middle of the street. I told the dispatcher to make the proper notifications. Once I arrived, there was a large tree down in the street. I placed police tape around the area because people will walk in the area and cars will come down the street even though they see the tree down. Now this middle-aged white couple was walking down the street and saw the downed tree. They said, "We love trees," and then walked by the police tape and started to stroke the tree as if it were a cat or pet. My attention had been turned to a motorist asking for directions. When I turned back around, I saw this couple petting this tree. I told them, "Get away from the tree." Then they asked me, "Don't you love trees?" I said to myself, *There is no way this just happened. Am I in the twilight zone?* I had to make sure I was awake. Was this a dream? No, it wasn't. All I could say was, "What the fuck?"

Here are some more shenanigans from white people. I responded to a robbery in progress. When I arrived, I found the complainant, a black male, and asked him to give me a description of the suspects. He wasn't able at the time, but you know who was able to provide me with the information? Whitey. Whitey stopped and gave me the description of all four suspects and their travel of direction. I was able to broadcast a lookout for the suspects. He then offered to get in my cruiser and ride around so we could identify them. We conducted an area canvass with negative results. He was instructed to wait until a detective arrived on the scene. Whitey said he lived in the neighborhood and didn't want people to see his face and know he was involved. Well guess what, hero? Too late for that. Since you wanted to be Mr. Helper, you are now a material witness; you go nowhere. Now he had Becky with him (Becky is a name I call white females). She started crying because they couldn't go. I'm looking at them like, *What is your problem? You wanted to get involved. Now you don't want to not be involved. The simple solution is, don't get involved.* By the way, the robbery was some bullshit.

Myself and another officer responded to a burglar alarm. When we arrived on the scene, we took the stairs to the office where the alarm was sounding. A white male came out and immediately asked, "How did you get up here?" He said it as if he was shocked that we made it to the second level. The other officer said, "Yeah, we spouted wings and floated up this mutha fucka, what do you mean how did we get up here, you idiot?" Of course, I kept a straight face but I couldn't contain it for very long. You should have seen the look on whitey's face. His mouth dropped and then he said, "I didn't mean it like that." I was saying to myself, *Yeah, right.*

Here's another one. We were working a local—that's a fire. The fire department was already on scene putting the fire out. Our job was to block the streets so no traffic came on the block.

Now, I had people inside of houses coming outside asking me if it was okay to come out. Keep in mind they were already outside and I hadn't said anything to them. A woman stood there and looked at the fire and asked, "Is it safe to go back inside?" I responded by saying, "Ma'am, if there is a problem we will let you know." Furthermore, I said, "You were already inside of the house." She said, "You don't have to make me feel stupid." I responded, "You did that all by yourself."

Why it is white people call us after they realize someone has attempted to break into their residence? I responded to a call for a burglary report. When I arrived on scene, I spoke with the complainant, who was a white female. I asked her, "What happened?" She told me someone attempted to break into her house the night before. I asked her if she had been inside. She said, "Yes." I asked, "Did you see him?" She said, "Yes." I asked, "Did you call 911?" She said, "No." I asked, "Why?" She said she didn't know what to do. Then she asked me, "What should have been done?" *Umm, I don't know, maybe call the police.* I'm saying to myself, *What the fuck is wrong with you?* Wow.

Now, white men think they are so smart; they love to talk down to police officers—especially black officers. So I play the game for a while. For instance, on a traffic stop, when I pull you over, it's not because I'm doing it just to do it, it's because you have committed a violation. This is the example: usually a young white guy gets pulled over, really for anything. The first thing to come out of his mouth is, "I work for Congressman or Senator whoever." My response is, "I'm officer Mac. License, registration, and proof of insurance, sir. The reason I'm stopping you is... you know the rest." Why is it he likes to get shitty with you? Then, when you write him the ticket, he always says, "I want to talk to your supervisor." I will call for an official, but many times before, I will tell him, "You want to talk to a supervisor, the district is over there." Of course I would like to say, "Hey, asshole, take your fucking ticket and shut your mouth." Now when this goes to court because he likes to contest tickets, he loses. Now, not only did he have to take off of work, he had to pay for parking to sit in Bureau of Traffic Adjudication for two or three hours, and then on top of that lose his case and had to pay the fine and/or loss of points on his license. Look, white man, you're not that smart. If you were, you'd know better than to challenge the police, especially when you are wrong. Listen, we have the authority to take away your freedom, but furthermore, we have the authority to take your life. So act right. I know what some white people are saying right now. *Who does this nigger think he is?* My question to you is Who do you think you are?

There's nothing more comical than seeing a white person locked up in front of a bunch of citizens. You want to talk about getting red in the face. I laugh like shit. It's funny to me. First thing he asks is, "Can I call my attorney?" I say, "Nope. Call him from jail," and I close the car door.

Another thing I have noticed is the amount of white people who are on some anti-depressant, or some other anti-anxiety medication mixed with pain-killing medication. The reason I know this is I have talked to pharmacists in the past. Of course, they can't tell me what individuals are taking, but they have told me what groups of people use. I was told that white people take all the anti-depressants available. Also, they take pain-killers. For sexual relations, they take herpes medication.

Now back to the anti-depressants. I always wondered why white people were so jipper. They are always smiling and happy. I'll bet if they stop taking their meds, they will be jumping off of bridges, roof tops, and taking their guns and killing people (and then themselves), as many have done in the past. Is it that bad, whitey, that you can't deal with reality? Is life that difficult for you? I have been on numerous calls when a white person has attempted to commit suicide. All I know is that if you apply some stress to a white person, he loses his mind. White people can't handle stress very well. Let someone say you're fired or anything that can cause a stressful situation. Guess what outcome the guns and now we have in an active shooter situation?

Want me to tell you what you white people know? You know what you see on TV, what you read in the papers, what you know on your jobs, and what you do with your friends, and that is the extent of what you know. Anything outside of that, and you're stuck. You don't have any common sense; all you have is book knowledge, and nothing more.

I'm writing all this not to be smart, but to ask some basic

questions out of curiosity. Where did this lack of common sense come from? Birth, inheritance, a learned environment, or from God who couldn't give you everything, since you have stolen everything else? Someone asked me if I like white people. I said, "Hell yeah,I like em, depends on how you cook 'em. but I like 'em. I mean, I like mine flame broiled."

Chapter Three
Bitches

The groups I will discuss next are black and white bitches. Black bitches first. Now, I have been on this earth for 41 years, and I have not seen anything like this before. This is not a put down, but an assessment of black bitches. What I've observed over the past 10 years in the DMV with black bitches are their attitudes. To say the least, I'm disappointed in what I've observed. Some of these bitches are so ghetto some are not. It is as if these women have to be the dominant ones in a relationship. They have become masculine, will talk back and say disrespectful things, and many of them have had children by two or three different men and dated drug dealers, but are educated; they just have no common sense. They are educated fools. Most of these women define themselves by their education or the materialistic items they have acquired. I'm talking these women went to universities for their bachelors', masters', and PhDs. With that being said, they lack character. What I'm seeing is a societal and educational brainwashing of this group. This is a sign of mental weakness.

For those of you who don't know, DC has the highest HIV rate in the nation. The majority of the affected population are the black women. This is how the majority of black women contract HIV. This is from what I know. These women date drug dealers who were in prison for an extended period of time. Now one of the drug boys has been in prison and has been raped by some nigga who has HIV. When that drug boy gets out, he's right back on the block.

Now these women know he's been incarcerated, but black bitches like this nigga because he has mad swagger or he has some money stashed away. So these two go back and smash; now this bitch contracts the virus. This woman likes to go to clubs; she is a groupie. She likes money. Therefore, ballplayers and drug dealers are her targets.

Women in the DC area are party women for the most part. DC is a party area. Give these women some weed, coke, or alcohol, and they are yours. It seems many of these women don't want a relationship; they just want to smash. There is nothing wrong with that. But they always complain about finding a good black man.

How can you say you want a good guy when you are not good yourself? But we must define what is good to them. You must understand they are conditioned. Many of these black women come from single parent households, consisting of the mother only. If you refer back to the chapter on *Niggaz vs. Black Folks*, you will understand. These women have not had a male figure in their lives for the most part. If so, the mother has had several different niggaz running in and out of her life. Therefore, they can't say they want a good man. What is a good man? No black woman can define a good man. Their definitions vary. You say you want a good man but you're jacked up yourself. Maybe an uncle or a grandfather is someone they looked up to. The black bitch really hasn't had any guidance on how to be a lady or a woman. You have other bitches who aren't worth a shit telling you how to accomplish something and they haven't accomplished anything. It's the blind leading the blind. Where are you learning to be a woman? At universities? Social gatherings? Who do these women have to look up to? Keep in mind, these mothers are in their teens and having children. I'm talking about 13 and up having children. How can you raise a child when you're 15 and your mother is 30? The grandmother is 48 or 50. One can see the dysfunction in this. But dysfunction is the norm in DC. Most of all, it's accepted.

Before I share some of my experiences, I would like to share a story. I went into a coffee shop and happened to notice a young lady I knew. I knew her from receiving calls for service at her residence. Now my first encounter with her was when she was 16. She was now 21, and I hadn't seen her for sometime. But when I would see her, I would ask her how she was doing in school. Is she going on to college? If not, is she going to get a trade? She would tell me, "Mac, I' m going to school after I graduate." I told her, "Great. Keep up the good work, and don't let anyone stop you from pursuing what you want in life."

When I saw her in the coffee shop, she was eight months pregnant. I asked her if she was ready to be a mother. She said, "Yeah." I asked her what the father did for a living. She said he worked a security job. I asked, "He's not a drug boy is he?" She said, "No, Mac, he isn't." I asked, "Did he finish high school?" She said, "No. He's getting his General Education Diploma (GED)." I asked her if they were going to live together. Her response was they were going to get an apartment. I asked her how they were going to afford it. She said, "He works." I asked her if she was working. She said, "No." She said she was on public assistance. She did have a job doing hair, but she didn't like it. She said she was thinking about going into the military. I asked her, "who was going to take care of the child when she went to basic training and advanced training." She asked, "The baby can't come with me?" She then told me, "The father will take care of the baby." I asked her if she had talked this over with him. She said, "No."

I asked how she got pregnant. She told me she was on the pill but missed it for a few days. I said, "Okay." I also inquired about her morals and values. She asked what I meant exactly. I then asked her about family structure. She asked, "What's that?" She said, "Mac, we grew up in two different generations. We see things totally different." I said, "I guess we do." The point I'm making is, this young lady is going to have a child. She has no concept of family structure, morals, or values. Now, what do you think her child is going to be like? As I said, the cycle perpetuates itself. I hope I'm wrong, but I've seen this too many times before. This young woman is setting this child up for failure even before the child is born.

As I stated earlier, I wanted to share some of my experiences with dating black bitches. This is why I don't date these bitches anymore. I met this woman at a gym. She had one hell of a body. She approached me and we started talking. We went out one night to dinner. I drove; it was a nice time. She told me I was direct and wasn't pretentious. As the date went on, she told me that she had a master's degree. I thought, *Wow*. At that time, I was impressed with all of that bullshit. We spent some time together, getting to know each other. We went to the movies, went shopping together, I always went to her house. Now, this is where it starts to get crazy. She asked me to grow a bush. A bush is a certain hairstyle for black men. I asked, "Why?" She said she liked that hairstyle.

As time went on, she eventually told me that she wanted to see another guy. I said, "Okay, that's fine." She went on to tell me that he was a professional basketball player. She said this guy had a bush. Then she said, "I met him before at a party, but he didn't want me." She said, "He's also married, but those guys have mistresses." I asked her if she wanted to be a mistress. She said she didn't care. I asked her, "Didn't he say he didn't like you or want you?" She said, "Yeah." I asked her about her self-esteem and her pride. She said those were irrelevant. She said that her feelings for him were interfering with our relationship. I said, "Whatever." Then she told me I was a gentleman. "Is that a bad thing?" I responded. She said with me it sometimes was. She said, "I know I'm fucked up. My morals and values are gone." I was like, *Really?* I was like, "You're just a fucked up person." She said, "I know." That was my first introduction to black bitches in the DMV.

I was talking to this brown-skinned black woman; she was attractive. She used to run track in college. She had a master's and worked for an engineering company. I met her at my friend's restaurant. We had good conversation. I observed she liked to drink a lot. When I asked her about her drinking habits she said she only drank wine. Well, that was not the truth, because she would have some hard drinks as well. I said, "Okay." If you tell me that you only drink wine and I see you drink something more, I know there is more to come. I was joking when I asked her, "How many drug dealers have you dated?" She said, "One." I was like, *Really, this is not surprising.* She told me when she was in college she dated this guy. I said, "This was some street dealer." She said no, and that he was pushing major weight. I then saw her car, a 2008 Mercedes Benz. She then told me how she acquired the car. She told me she met a guy on somethingDaddy.com. The guy she was dating bought it for her. I was like, *Okay*. Well, let's see, she's drunk and a whore. Perfect. So we went out. I was like, *What surprise is next?* Although, as a police officer, nothing should surprise you about people.

When she picked me up, she had a glass of wine on the center console. I was like, "Are you serious?" She said, "Okay, baby, I'll pour it out." Then she said, "I'm still somewhat drunk." I said, "Okay, I'll drive." On our way, she asked me whether it was safe with me being a police officer. I asked her what she meant. She said she was concerned because I carried my gun. I asked her whether she was safe with a drug dealer as a boyfriend.

Remember, their competition wants to rub them out. If she was with him then she was a target as well. I'm saying to myself, *She is an idiot.*

When we arrived at our destination we did have a good time. Although, she told me she drank only wine, but she had multiple glasses of beer. I was like, "You told me you drank only wine." She said, "I'm not perfect." I said, "Really?" Then she told me she had a kid but was not ready to be a mother. I asked her, "How does that work?" She said, "I'm not ready." Then I asked her if the kid was from the guy on the website. She said no. She said, "I was seeing another guy and got pregnant while I was seeing the guy on the website." All I could say was, "Wow."

This other woman I was talking to had a PhD in education. She was very attractive and from DC. We went out a few times and I asked her if she was seeing anyone. She told me no. The reason I ask this question is that sometimes people are possessive and when men hit the ass a few times they think it's theirs. As a police officer, I don't want some crazyass watching her and me while we are out. Well, that's what happened. This guy she said she wasn't seeing saw us out. Don't you know this fool was crazy? We were at a restaurant in Maryland and this guy passed the table twice. My radar went up and I asked her if she knew this guy. She said, "No." He passed for a third time and said, "I thought you were sick." I said, *Here we go.* All I could think of was, don't let this fool have a gun. Because this shit happens all the time, of course I carry my gun, because you don't know what people are going to do. Now, I started to pull my gun out of my holster just waiting for this guy to make some sort of motion toward his waistline. If he did, he was as good as dead. She told him she didn't have to tell him anything. She could do what she wanted. Now I was caught in the middle of this. All I could do was get up and say I had to go to the bathroom, which I did. After I returned from the bathroom, I told her I would be right back. I went straight to my SUV and left her at the restaurant.

That's the type of shit that could have ended tragically for both of them. Because if he would have made a move for his waistline, I would have turned him into a sprinkler system. Then, I would have shot her dumb ass for getting me caught up in some stupid shit like that. This is why cops are leery of black bitches and niggaz. Just going out can be problems with people. Only because you really don't know who you are dating and if what they are telling you is the truth.

What people fail to understand is that you, the citizen, can pretty much do what you want. I can't. The things you can do, I can't. If you get arrested, you don't have to worry about losing your job, house, or anything. I do. So pretty much everything I've worked for can be taken away in a matter of minutes. Well, she left a message on my cell phone the next day apologizing for the incident. She said, "You left me at the restaurant and I had to take a cab home." Needless to say, I didn't return the call.

Another young lady I met also had a master's and was very

accomplished in her professional career. She was a director of an agency. She also had a Mercedes Benz. We went out. We had a great time together. She asked me why I carried my firearm off-duty. To her, it was an act of insecurity. I am an active shooter instructor and a tactical team instructor. For those of you who don't know, a tactical team instructor is a SWAT instructor. I know better than to leave the house without my firearm. That's because our society has become increasingly violent. Active shooter situations can occur any place at any time. It's better to have that firearm than not to have it. I told her, "The next person who comes into the restaurant, tell me what he's thinking." She said, "I'm not a mind reader." I said, "That's why I carry this gun off-duty. What if that person decided to come in and just start shooting?" Her response was, "Then if that's what God wants." She said, "I couldn't stop that." I'm looking at her like, *What the fuck?* I realize how a cop's mentality is different from the average everyday person. I'm thinking to myself, *If I listen to this bitch, she will get me killed.* As a black woman, I expected her to have more sense than this.

When I called the next day, the conversation started out well. Then I asked her some questions about her sorority, like the history and what was the mindset? She then went on the defensive and said, "That's not a normal question, and normal people don't ask or say things like that." Okay. I asked if it was normal to divulge personal information about two previous abortions when I barely know you. "Is that normal?" She then said, "You're insecure and I don't want to talk to you anymore." I said, "Okay." Then I talked to someone who worked in the field and knew her. I was informed by that person that she was as crazy as a loon. This person told me anyone as accomplished as she was and who had not been married at her age had a problem. The person then told me, "Yeah, she's fine, but her ass is crazy." This person continued to tell me how she said she had ghosts running around her house. I said, "Wow."

I met this one at a restaurant; she was light-brown-skinned with a beautiful body. We talked for a little while, exchanged numbers, and went out. When we went to eat and our meals arrived, she asked me if she could taste my food. I said, "Sure." She said my food was good. Before I could begin to eat my dinner, she asked for another taste. I said, "Okay." I asked her if she liked it that much. She said, "Yeah." As we ate, she ate her dinner and kept picking at mine. Now I started to get pissed. I asked her, "Didn't you get enough to eat?" She said, "Yeah, but yours is really good." I told her to eat her meal and leave mine alone. She said I was selfish. I told her she was greedy. As the night ended and I dropped her off. I asked her if she had a good time. She said, "Yes." I was like, *Good.* I told her, "Goodnight," and she got out of my car. I told myself, *Fuck that; that bitch tried to eat up my dinner. That won't happen again.*

This black woman I met at a local store. I went in to buy something before I went to work out. Later on in the afternoon, I saw her again. So we talked for a minute and exchanged numbers. She kept saying I was "stalking her." Okay, ladies and gentleman, that's a red flag for cops. Now this woman was from the DMV; she worked for the government. She was 5'9", 160 lbs, and thick. She had a master's degree as well. When I called her, I asked her why she said I was stalking her. She said it was a joke. Then I saw her again, same place, same location. She said, "This means something." I said, "It means we live in the same vicinity and shop at the same place. What's the big deal? It's nothing more than that." So we started talking, she would call me, and I would be as nice as I could be without offending her. I could tell she was delicate. I'm not so nice. I'm direct and to-the-point. She told me she wanted a relationship. I told her, "I don't even know you. Why don't we get to know each other first?" I asked her what she liked to do. She said she liked to go to Baltimore on the harbor. I said, "That's cool. What else do you like to do?" She said she liked to hang out and read. "That's cool," I responded. I asked her, "Why are you not seeing anyone?" She told me, "Men are hard to find; at least good men." Bottom line, we really didn't connect. The reason we didn't connect was I could tell she wanted a relationship and was trying to push it upon me. Not only that, she started to annoy me by asking me the most simple questions. I'm the mental type. A woman has to stimulate me intellectually to keep my interest, now that I'm older. Yeah, being nice-looking is one thing, but that wears off quickly with me.

This one relates to a young mother of four with two different fathers. This woman lived in DC. I went to pick her up. We were out for a little, and I was just joking when I asked to see her ass. She said, "Okay," reclined the seat in my SUV, pulled her pants down, and turned over. I was like, "Dayum." She said, "Is this what it's about? If it is, then you should pay me." I said, "So you're a prostitute?" She said, "No, but if you want to fuck, then I want something."

I said, "Wow." With the HIV rate the way it is in DC, I would be out of my mind to even think about having sex with this woman.

This young lady I met while she was finishing work on her PhD. This black woman attended a university in DC. She was attractive, 5'8", brown-skinned, about 150 pounds. I met her while working out at a gym. We went out for a while. I remember one day we had a disagreement. I told her she should leave. She told me she was going to call my agency and tell them I hit her. My heart started beating about 400 beats per minute; that's the kiss of death for a police officer—domestic violence. Cops don't ever joke about that. I told her, "Stay away from me."

That's why cops are so hesitant about dating black women. In fact, that was a power move on her part. She knew just by filing a complaint I would get in trouble. Then the next day she called to apologize. She left a message on the answering machine. I didn't answer the phone nor did I talk to her again. Approximately six years later we saw each other again. I asked her how things were going. She said, "Okay," and then she looked like she was about to cry. She told me sometime after we broke up that she was living with this guy and the guy was on the down low. For those of you who don't know, this is a guy who is bi-sexual or gay. He hides the fact that he also likes men from his female partner. Now she told me that there was the possibility that he could have infected her with the HIV. This woman was extremely arrogant and thought her shit didn't stink. Well, she was humbled while we talked. When she attempted to hug me, I pulled away. I was thinking,

No more black women for me. That shook my tree all too well.

I was at a restaurant talking to two black females. They worked for the federal government and had bachelors' degrees. As we discussed what they did for a living, I was interrupted with a phone call. One of the females said, "You speak Spanish." I said, "I do speak Spanish, but that wasn't Spanish." She asked what it was. I said, "You tell me." Not one of the two could figure out the language. As the conversation continued, the discussion was about black women from the DMV. I said, "They have a reputation for being ghetto." The one asked me where I was from. I told her, "New Jersey." She said, "They're ghetto in NJ." I said, "Not as ghetto as the people from the DMV." She said, "DC women are ghetto. Women from Maryland are classy." I asked, "What about the women from Baltimore? Are they classy?" Then she had the nerve to tell me she was classy. I said, "Classy? Are you serious?" Listen, if any one woman has to tell you she is classy, it's the complete opposite. I asked her, "Is that tattoo on your chest, is that classy? What about the one on your wrist, is that classy too? What about the two tats on your fingers, are those classy as well?" I said, "Classy, that's some gangsta shit." I asked her if she was a gangsta bitch. Then I talked about her gear. She was trying to be sexy. That's all good, but the gear she had on made her look like a whore. As they finished dinner, they asked me if I was going be a gentleman and walk them to their car. I told them, "Hell no." They both told me I was mean and left the restaurant.

I'm saying this to say, even though the ratio of women to

men in the DC area is 10 to 1, this is the reality of it. Three of the 10 are going to have HIV or some form of a sexually-transmitted disease. Three more are going to have two or three children by two different fathers. Two more are going to be lesbians. One of the two is going to be emotionally unstable (crazy). The last one you just hope you are compatible with.

My point is, just because you have an education, doesn't make you a good catch. Many times black women are influenced by reality television, fictional books, and ridiculous ghetto magazines. This is mindless entertainment. The educated black women read and watch this too. Are your lives that boring? Or has society gone downhill that much? It's both. What I've learned from my experiences while dealing with the sophisticated black bitch is they are not shit. All the education and materialistic items they have is a mask for how jacked up they really are. As I said earlier, they think that their education defines who they are. These are the biggest frauds I have seen. What these females lack is good character.

The next section deals with police confrontations with black women. Before I start, I have one question to ask: What makes black women think they can say and do what they want as if there won't be any consequences for their actions?

The first situation I wanted to bring attention to is the officer in Seattle who struck that black girl in her face. As a police officer, I'm telling you that strike was a justified strike. I'm sure based upon his training and the law there was nothing wrong with what the officer did. I know many people in the black community were pissed off. I don't understand why. Listen, it's this simple, don't put your hands on a police officer when he's attempting to arrest another individual; then you don't have to worry about getting punched. I'll bet she won't do that ever again. The black community said the officer should not have hit a woman. Are you serious, black community? Look, you lose the title of woman, lady, or whatever when you start fighting with the police. Her new title became combatant.

The next one deals with a traffic stop. The officer asked the lady for her license, registration, and insurance information. She complied, and he ran her information. She was driving on a suspended license. The officer returned to her vehicle, and told her she was driving on a suspended license. The officer told her to step out of the vehicle; she asked what for, and then got on her cell phone to call someone. The officer told her again. Now that the female was non-compliant, the officer pulled his taser and commanded her to get out of the car. She said no. He used the taser. She got cooked for a little bit but complied after the cooking. She was arrested. Now why didn't she just follow the officer's lawful order to exit the vehicle? All of this could have been avoided if that woman would have done what she was told to do.

These are multiple police encounters I've had with black women. I was driving, and this car crossed the double yellow line. On this street, there is one lane each way—one lane traveling northbound, the other traveling southbound. The tags were also expired. I pulled her over. I asked her for her license, registration, and proof of insurance, and explained to her why I stopped her. I told her: 1) for the traffic violation and 2) the tags were expired. She said she wasn't showing me anything. I told her to step out of the car. She refused. I then asked for an additional unit to assist me. Another officer arrived and assisted me with taking the female out of the car. As I escorted the female back to my cruiser, she pulled away from me and squared off and threw a punch. She missed; I didn't. She was bounced off the front of my cruiser and went to the ground. She began yelling and screaming for help. As she was crying, she was still resisting our efforts to handcuff her. She was eventually handcuffed and charged with the two violations and assault on a police officer. I remember a man who witnessed the incident said, "She will never do that again. I'll guarantee it."

The second incident: I was on traffic stop, a car approached, me and the female, who was a nigga, said her baby's father was after her. At the same time, another car approached and this nigga jumped out. I told him to come over to the side of the road. He became very agitated and aggressive. So for his safety and mine I attempted to handcuff him. He didn't want to be handcuffed, so he started to fight. Then the passenger in the car, who was his new girlfriend, exited the vehicle and jumped on my back. Now I was fighting with two people. I attempted to call an additional unit, but my mic was knocked from my shoulder from the female on my back. I had to knock this bitch off of my back. When I didn't acknowledge my radio after several attempts from the dispatcher because I was on traffic stop and fighting, they sent additional officers to my location. But some citizen also called 911, stating a police officer was in a fight. Two or three units arrived in seconds, but I was fighting for two minutes. Needless to say, the female went to the hospital. Both were charged with assault on a police officer.

The third incident occurred when it was almost time for check-off. Check-off is when the officer's tour has ended. I was driving, and a group of black bitches were on the street. I told the one young black woman to stand back on the curb and not to stand on the street. One stated, "You can't tell me what to do." I stopped my cruiser and told her, "Back on the curb! You're going to obstruct traffic." She told me I was just a civilian and I had no authority. I told her to get on the curb. She was like, "What are you going to do?" She then explained she had a 3.9 grade point average at her university and was an honor grad. I said, "So?" She then went on to say that we have a new black president and I shouldn't be like this, and can't we all just get along? I said, "No, we can't." I just obtained information from her. Then she said to me, "You just wanted to know my name." What I really wanted to do was snatch that wig she was wearing off of her head. But I was just like, "What the fuck?"

There are so many stories, but I'll just tell one more to make my point. We received a call for a disorderly female. She became more belligerent with the other officer I was working with, and she was placed under arrest. When we placed her in the back of the cruiser, she twisted her lower half and kicked me right in the chest. I felt like I was in the *Matrix*. One arm went back and then the other. I then heard on the radio that she APO'd (assaulting a police officer) Mac. Well, when we got her back to the station, this bitch started to undress in the cellblock. I mean, she was butt naked. I was like, *What the fuck?* My point is, these bitches think they can do what they want. What they really need is a good ass-kicking. Violence is a behavior modification tool. When applied appropriately, it works.

Here are some more examples not related to anything above. These are just observations I've made while at work. I was at eating a restaurant; two black women came and asked the hostess if they could be seated. The hostess told them it was going to be a little while. The black woman said, "I want to eat now," and walked past the hostess to find a table. I'm looking at this woman like, *Are you smoking crack?* The hostess called to the woman and said there were no tables. This black woman said, "Bitch, I want a table now." The hostess called the owner over. The owner was very nice. As a matter of fact, he was overly nice. He told the lady, "Have patience." The next table would be for her. He then told her she and her friend could sit at the bar until a table was ready. The woman calmed down and had a few drinks.

Every Friday night this restaurant has a party. It's nothing but blacks and niggaz mixed. I know the niggaz when they come in. I also know the blacks. Now there was a group of ghetto bitches sitting at the bar eating wings and French fries. There is nothing wrong with eating wings and fries except I heard Lecrecia, "Dem wings is good, ain't dey, gurl?" I cringed, and then one of the bitches began to suck and pick her teeth with her fingernail. I said to myself, *Are you serious?* I just stared at them.

This is the last example; I was at a restaurant when three black women, dressed nicely, entered the restaurant. They sat down and ordered some wine. Now the one bitch thought she was classy, crossed her legs, and sat there drinking her wine and attempted to order more wine from the list. They started a conversation with me. They asked me if I was allowed to be in a restaurant. My response was, "I can eat too." Then one of the women said I had a smart mouth and didn't want to talk to me. I was like, "Good, then I can eat in peace." But the one who had her legs crossed engaged me in conversation. She said she was a paralegal and worked for a large firm. I asked where she was from? She said DC. She told me she attended a university in Maryland. I said, "Good." She went on to tell me that both her parents were drug abusers and she shouldn't have made it this far in life. I asked her, "Why?" She told me all the things that she had been through and how she really didn't have a strong family structure but she said she made it. She was proud of her accomplishment. I was too. As I said, I'm big on education, but I'm bigger on character. She then asked me if I had attended a university. I told her, "Yes." I had a bachelor of arts and at the time was working on my master's. She was like, "And you are a cop?" I said, "Yeah." I asked her, "Because I'm a cop do you think my IQ drops 50 points just because?" Then she attempted to challenge me intellectually; bad move on her part, because she was a pseudo-intellectual. After I got done with this bitch, she didn't know what to say. I pretty much humiliated her. She told me she liked the challenge. I told her, "It wasn't much of one." We then started to talk about black women and how messed up they are. All three of the women jumped me at once. As we discussed our differences, I brought up lack of character. The one who engaged me the most said, "I don't know what character is, but I have lots of it." I said, "Right." I told her she was a joke.

I have noticed after dealing with these so-called sophisticated black bitches, they are no different than the street bitch. All they have is more education, better clothes, a nice car, better jobs, and better homes. The games are still the same. They love to play games. For what reason I have no clue. I think games are for common people. For the most part after playing games and spending time with that sophisticated black bitch, you find out she is some boo-boo. Guess what, guys? You have wasted your time.

My advice is directed to the so-called sophisticated, educated, black bitch. Stop pretending to be something that you are not and accept your role and status in life as a hoe, fool, or stupid bitch. This is what men say and feel. You are what you are—a bitch. Now, what the fuck?

White bitches: I really can't say too much about them. It seems they know their place. They won't argue with their men in public. They are also somewhat easier to get along with than black bitches. I have noticed in the Capitol Hill area of DC they think they are entitled to certain things. They act like the world belongs to them. I laugh at Becky. She thinks she's smart but she's a dummy. No common sense. I see these white bitches get taken to the bank all the time. These dudes they mess around with play the shit out of them. I've seen these white bitches walk around on 8th St. S.E. in the summer with a short skirt and no panties. They'll walk over a grate that has air blowing upward and when they cross the grate, their dresses blow up and there are their asses. Then they look to see if anyone saw it. *Bitch, you did that intentionally.* Then they try to look embarrassed with a big smile on their face. So when you get raped by some niggaz or Billy—that's what I call the WB's white boys—don't say shit. You invited it. I guess those anti-depressants have quite an effect on the mind. Maybe it's the other drugs you use—cocaine, ecstasy, and others that make you feel invincible. My question is to white bitches: What makes you think you are entitled to anything? For example, there was a white bitch who came into the station to file a complaint. She said she didn't like the way the officer talked to her. She was asked, "What did he say?" She couldn't articulate anything, but she said she didn't like the way he spoke to her. I'm there in the next room listening to this white bitch. All I'm thinking is that if I were out there, I would say something like, "Is this the way you would like to be spoken to, your royal highness, oh ye fair maiden, for thou art wrong for your mistreatment? I implore you for your forgiveness." Is that better? Now get the fuck out of the station, bitch.

I was talking to this white bitch in a restaurant. Our conversation was about Washington, DC and Capitol Hill. As our conversation progressed, she said, "The holidays were a peaceful time." I asked, "According to whom?" She said, "No violence happens on the holidays." I said, "Really? I beg to differ." I explained to her that most homicides, suicides, and acts of domestic violence happen during the holidays. She said I was a liar. I asked her how she knew. I told her to show me what she knew based upon her experiences. She didn't have a response. Then she said the police were crazy. I replied with, "We respond to your craziness." Then she said, "Oh, no, you are negative." I asked her how I was negative. She responded by telling me I separated the police from the citizens. I said, "We are separate." She said, "You are too negative." I explained to her the truth is the truth. What I see and deal with on a daily basis is not what she deals with. She was so upset, she said, "I'm done talking to you." I told her, "Then keep it moving." She left the restaurant.

I was standing in front of a Dunkin' Donuts and a canine police car was behind me. Two bitches approached me—one black and one white. They came up to me and asked if that was a dog in the back of the cruiser. I said, "No, ladies. Our agency no longer uses dogs. That is a Bengal Tiger in the back of the vehicle." Of course the entire time I kept a straight face. Then I told them I was joking. I said, "Yes, that's a dog in the back." I then said, "But our agency is only permitted to use male dogs." They said, "No female dogs?" I said, "No, ladies." They asked, "Why?" I explained to them, during training with male and female dogs, that the female dogs were not trainable because they lacked reasoning skills. Therefore, we were not permitted to use female dogs. For those of you who don't get it, bitches lack reasoning skills.

Chapter Four
Faggots

I'm not here to write about the men who have alternative lifestyles and are quiet and discreet. I'm going to write about the flamers, the queens, and the flamboyant faggots. I see and deal with these weirdoes on a daily basis. My question is what makes a young or grown man want to act like a woman? This is some sick shit. I see them as young as 14 years old with their skinny jeans on switching around in DC. I see them walking around with their cut-off shirts and their arms up in the air waving their hands, carrying on. I'm like, *What the fuck?*

My friends who taught me to speak Arabic would fuck with them. They would say, "Luti mishnun," which, translated, means "crazy faggot" in Arabic. I wouldn't say anything. Just observe and shake my head. The thing that bothers me the most is their boldness in society. As I have said, I have traveled to the Middle East, South America, and Afghanistan. This type of behavior is not tolerated. In South America, they attempted to kill a pastor for trying to marry two homos. Furthermore, they love to hurt and kill fags in South America. In the Middle East and Afghanistan, Sharia law is practiced. I wish the homos in these countries would act like the homos in the United States. But you know what, they know better. You know why? Because in these countries they would be killed. People think twice before they start doing some crazy shit like these homos do in the United States. Homosexuality is not permitted outwardly in countries where Sharia law is practiced. So if you are a flamboyant ferry, stay your ass here in the United States.

What I have noticed is these other countries are conservative in their views, whereas we are very liberal. DC is a very liberal city. I would love to see the queens in the United States act like they do in the Middle East, Afghanistan, or South America. Death would be imminent. What I'm having trouble understanding is how it got this far. Why are teenage boys acting like women? This is just sick. The worst part about this is these are black males. On occasion, I will see a white homo act as stupid as the black homos. But the majority of fags I deal with are black. Throughout this chapter, I will give you examples of how bitches influence their boys to become feminine.

I remember I was called for a missing person; as usual, the mother had no idea where her son was. Of course, I asked the normal questions. Who does he hang out with? She said, "He hangs in another district," and actually gave an address. Well, I followed up and went to the address. But I asked how old her son was. She said, "Fifteen." How old is the person he hangs out with? She said, "Twenty-five." I said, "Twenty- five." I asked, "Why is a twenty-five-year-old man hanging out with a teenager?" She said she had no idea. I told the mother I thought she knew. When she told me he was twenty five, I knew he was turning this young boy out. I asked, "How often does he hang out with this man?" She said, often. I asked where the boy's father was. She said she didn't know. I asked, "Why are you not kicking his ass?" She said, "There's nothing I can do with him." As I stated earlier, the absence of the male figure in the household is rough. This boy is being taught to be a homo by a fucked-up individual who most likely went through the same process. Once again, if you read the chapters on *Niggaz vs. Black Folks* and *Bitches*, you will understand this better.

I was called to a home for a family disturbance; upon arrival there was a young black child misbehaving. The father had called and was concerned. The father had adopted this boy. The father was white and a homo and the father's boyfriend lived at the house as well. Now how can two white homos (or any homo) raise a child, black or white? This is the dysfunction I discuss all of the time. But I'm thinking to myself, there is nothing good that can come out of this situation. I'll bet within ten years, this kid will be one of those faggots walking around switching his ass. I will say this: there is some twisted shit that goes on in our society. These are things that I experience on a daily basis. These are things most people really don't hear or see.

I was serving warrants with another officer and we obtained information about the fugitives' whereabouts. When we went to the motel room, we knocked, announced, and said, "Police."

When the one male answered the door, we said we had a warrant for the individual. There were what appeared to be two females in the bed. This was until they got out of the bed. What I thought were two women were actually two men. They were wearing wigs and had tits and dicks. I thought I was getting ready to throw up. Then there was the smell. Oh, the smell. It smelled like ass and dick. My partner was like, “Mac, are you okay?” I said, “No.” After we handcuffed the wanted fugitive, I had to step outside and get some air. The other men had no wants or warrants; they were let go. I told my partner, “This was the sickest thing I‘ve seen since I’ve been on the job.” As I stated, I’ve seen people with their brains spattered on the ground, people burned beyond recognition, and people in accidents decapitated. But that shit with the homos made my stomach churn.

An officer and I were assigned to a hospital detail, and on the way we were flagged down. I told him to keep driving, and that we needed to get to the hospital detail. The reason I knew it was some bullshit was because there were a bunch of flaming black faggots flagging us down. So, disregarding my advice, this stupid officer stopped. I told him, “Since you stopped, you handle this.” He was like, “No problem.” When my partner got out of the car the first thing the faggots said was that the other two black men called them faggots and showed them knives. Now we had a problem, because if there were knives involved this would become an arrestable offense. Well, come to find out there were no knives involved. But the faggots complained and said, “They called us faggots.” I just stood there and listened to this bullshit. Then they said they wanted a police report. If we didn't do a police report they would talk with the Gay Action Network and file a complaint. My partner looked at me, I looked at him, and I told him to handle it. The last thing you want to get is a complaint from the gay community. So my partner took all of their information and told them he would file a report. Of course, he didn't, and they didn't ask for report numbers. When he got back in the car he said, "I shouldn't have stopped." I was like, "No shit, retard."

I was in a cruiser with another officer and there was this homo crossing the street. I said to the officer, "Blow your horn at him. Let's see what he does." So the officer hits the air horn. This fag turns, looks, and blows us a kiss. The officer and I turned and looked at each other. We then at the same time said, "What the Fuck?" and started laughing. I said, "Dude, this city is off the fucking chain." I said it was only a joke, but when he did that I was like, "Great googalie moogalie."

I was working mandatory overtime and a call came out for a suspicious vehicle. Since the vehicle was in an alley, I drove in from the rear of the location with another officer. There was a black male in the car. He said he was waiting for his girlfriend. We said, "Okay." When his girlfriend came out, she had long hair, tits, and a bone structure like a man. The officer I was with asked to see her identification. It was actually a man. This is how these nastyass people get the HIV and pass it on. I started to feel ill and told the officer we should go. I then told him, "These are some worthless fucks."

I was at my friend's restaurant and on certain Saturdays it's boy's night. That's code for fag night. Now keep in mind this whole section is about the queens and flamers. On those certain Saturdays you will not catch me anywhere near his restaurant. But one day, two of the flamers came in. They were telling people about how they were eating each other's assholes and one shit in the other's mouth. When I heard this, I almost threw up. I got up from the bar where I was eating and left. I didn't even pay the bill. That's because the owner was my friend. But I told him about the incident, and he said they already told him. I asked him, "What the fuck is up with these weirdoes?" Now come on, people, that is some filthy shit. Now my friend knows I despise that type of behavior displayed by homos.

Another incident occurred at my friend's restaurant; he set me up. The owner and I were sitting downstairs eating dinner and the two homos showed up. He asked me if I wanted to go upstairs and finish eating. I said, "Sure." No more than ten minutes later, here come the fags. As I ordered some sushi, they came and sat two seats down from me. I was like, okay, what are they doing up here? As I was watching tennis on television and eating, one of the boys started talking about how he wanted to suck a tennis player's dick. He then said how he could lick this tennis player's asshole and said he hoped it wasn't hairy. He then went on to talk about how he shaved his pubic area and his asshole. I had enough. Matter of fact, I started to feel myself boil on the inside. I was like, "Enough, you mother fucker." I told him, "If you want to talk about that shit, do that around your other boys, not around me." He's lucky I'm a cop and not some guy who just had a gun. Because, if I wasn't a cop, it wouldn't have been a good night for those two. My friend set me up. He thought that was the funniest thing. He said, "You should have seen your face." Sometimes when I go to eat at the restaurant, the two boys will be in there. The one will stare at me, and if I walk by he'll hiss. I'm like, *You hissed at me. Hissing at people; what the fuck is that?* Of course, I'm supposed to accept that type of behavior. Right? Wrong; not me.

Now during Halloween, everyone was wearing his or her costumes. There was a big white faggot who came into the restaurant. I mean, he's at least 6'4" and weighs about 250 lbs. He came in dressed like a baby. He had on a bonnet, baby clothes, a diaper, and high-heeled shoes. He came in saying hi to everyone. I'm eating lobster tails and shrimp and I see this thing in blue walk by me. I was like, *Are you serious?* He bent over and started kissing people; he then floated out of the restaurant.

One of my sources informed me in general conversation about a homosexual who was hanging out around a certain group of military personnel in the area. This gay guy was drinking with the military guys and getting them drunk. After they were drunk, he would ask them if he could suck them off. According to my source, many of the military personnel would allow him to suck them off, and they have since turned into homosexuals. I'm like, *Wow*. As I said, this is the real world. Most people don't hear about this. But guess what? The streets are watching you. If you think you're not being watched, you are. Believe me.

The last story deals with a black homo who picked up another homo. According to him, he wanted to have fun. Well, the homo comes into the station to file a report. The report was for a sexual assault. He was interviewed and stated that he and this guy had sex. He then went on to say he wanted it was too rough and he was injured. He was asked how he was too rough. The fag described how the other one choked him and when he came to he was getting it in the ass. He was asked if he wanted any medical attention, by the officer conducting the interview. If so, we would have had to call the ambulance for a sexual assault victim. The ambulance would have had to check him out and take him to the hospital. Now, after telling this man (or whatever you want to call him) what had to be done for the procedure, he refused to file a police report. You wonder why cops look at you funny and never smile.

Chapter Five
DC as a Hole

First of all, I want to say the DMV is a great area. It has so much to do. There is so much history, so many places to eat; the variety of food is great. This area has some of the best universities. All the entertainment you want is here. There are so many different groups of people. Therefore, one must be culturally aware. This is a multi-cultural society. I have traveled all over the country and visited many Metropolitan areas, but I must say the DMV is one of the best. I will, however, say the people are somewhat different.

This is easily the craziest area I have worked in. There are more mental health cases here than I have seen before. The people are rude and obnoxious. They actually think they can do what they want. There is no respect for anything, anybody, or the law. People lack good morals and values. One would think that this is where the laws are made, so there would be some form of ethical conduct and people would follow the law. In fact, it's the complete opposite. These people are flagrant violators of the law. This is a corrupt area. Therefore, if you are not a crook or not somewhat dirty, you will be an outcast.

Anything and everything is out here and it has its price. Just because it's not in your face doesn't mean it doesn't exist. I want to discuss the mentally ill. As I stated in the first paragraph, there are tons of mentally ill in the Washington, DC area. I received numerous radio runs for people running in the middle of traffic, jumpers on bridges, people screaming at cars, running down the street butt naked and when you put them in the cruiser, they would shit or piss in your cruiser. There were many times I would see people walking down the street, just talking to themselves. These are blacks and whites together. I'm looking at these people and I'm wondering, *How did this happen? Are there not enough mental institutions in the area or is/was there not enough money to keep these people locked in their facility?* I'll give one example of what I mean.

I received a call for a woman who was talking to parked cars. I responded and asked the middle-aged white female what was wrong and how could I help her. She responded, "There is nothing wrong with me; I feel fine." I asked her why she was talking to cars parked in the street. She said, "I always do that." Then she said to me, "I also have plants growing out of my head; can you help me with this?" "Of course I can," I responded. I then got on my radio and asked the dispatcher for the number to the Department of Agriculture. I figure if this woman has plants growing out of her head, who better to assist her than the Department of Agriculture? I gave her the number and left.

As you know, the DMV is where all of the law-makers reside

for the United States, and of course, the District of Columbia. I was talking to one of my sources one day. He would tell me how these white boys would buy cocaine for parties and take the coke back to the hotels where high-level politicians and their staff members would hold their parties and have prostitutes. I was informed that there were a lot of alternative lifestyle activities at these parties. Some of the partygoers were bi-sexual or gay. They would have orgies and pour alcoholic beverages in the woman's vagina while she was doing a handstand and drink it out of her vagina. I was like, *Damn*. I knew people were jacked up, but what the fuck? Man never ceases to amaze me. Actually, nothing man does shocks me anymore.

During training we were shown videos of people on the Metro—that's the subway—being pushed down on the tracks and getting hit by the trains. The funny thing is, no one even thought to help the people who fell on the tracks. People were just standing around looking at the people get hit by the train. This, of course, should be troubling to any reader of this book. This is the reality as a police officer. Speaking of the Metro, there was a mother with a baby in a stroller and another infant or toddler on the escalator. Now the mother had moved ahead of the infant and was almost at the bottom. The infant or toddler had fallen and was going down the escalator. The kid's scared to death, and he's screaming because he's afraid. Don't you know nobody picked this little kid up? I did. You know why? Because if that were my kid I would want someone to help my child. But you yo-yos wouldn't even think of helping this child. I picked him up and he stopped crying. I took him to his mother and she said, "Thanks." Don't you know there was a female military officer at the bottom. She said, "Thank you for helping that child." My response was "Why didn't you help the child, instead of looking at him, stupid?" She just stared at me. Of course, I was in a suit because I just came from court. This way she could never file a complaint, and she had no idea I was a police officer. There are so many things that happen in DC that you never even hear about. To most people, if they don't hear about it, then it doesn't happen. Well guess what, people? Things you don't hear about still happen.

How many citizens live in their own little worlds? None of them have a clue about what's going on around them. If an officer tells someone do something, the citizen looks at the officer like he's stupid. For example, on a traffic post when the lights are out, why do citizens find it necessary to stop and ask questions? Okay, there is already a problem—the lights are out. Then you compound problems by stopping and asking questions. Drive your vehicle. Don't ask anything. Citizens will stop and ask what the problem is. I respond, "Well, the lights are out." Then they ask me, "How long is this going to take to fix?" Am I the light company? How would I know? Also, citizens will ask for directions; they will ask me where a particular place is. Then I tell them. They say, "I don't think that's right." Well since you know, why did you ask? Then they say, "My GPS tells me it's back there." I respond, "Then go back where the GPS tells you it is."

Many of you are laughing, but I'm talking about you. Most people want to rely on technology. It makes everything so simple. Well, citizens, what do you do when your technology fails? I know most people don't use MapQuest or even know how to read a map. You are shit out of luck when your GPS fails. Heaven forbid there is a street closure; a citizen will lose his or her mind. I remember I was parked in an alley with my cruiser because something had occurred. A citizen in his vehicle came up and asked me to move. I responded, "I'm conducting police business; you will have to find an alternate route." This individual said, "I live over there. How am I supposed to get home?" Now, a person with any amount of common sense would go around the block and enter his home. Not here, that's too difficult to do. Why are citizens stupid?

The DMV has the worst drivers in the country. I mean, they are terrible. I remember when it would rain, I would take a handful of accident reports with me because I knew there would be serious problems. Now knowing you can't drive, why do you compound matters by using a cell phone when driving? I love giving tickets for this moving violation, especially if you have the audacity to do this in front of me. Now put the two together: bad weather conditions and driving with a cell phone. All I can say is what the fuck? I know someone is going to the hospital if I get a call for an accident under these circumstances. When I get on the scene, I really want to say, "Can't you people drive?" But we already know the answer to that.

This is what many of the people do in DC. For example, if you call us, don't say there is a man with a gun just to make us get there faster. For us this is a priority call. Many police accidents happen on priority runs. For one, the citizens never pay attention when we have our emergency equipment activated. The citizens run into us. I'll give you two examples from personal experience. I was called for an assault in progress. This is a priority assignment. We had our lights and sirens activated. As we were driving, a car pulled out right in front of us. My partner attempted to avoid striking the vehicle but was not able to so. We struck the vehicle; hit a fire hydrant and a light pole. Now out of this, I injured my neck, back, received seven stitches over my eye, four stitches inside of my eye, and a concussion. My partner suffered a concussion and received numerous staples in his head to close a very large laceration he received from the accident. The car's engine was pushed back from the impact. Our vehicle was destroyed.

In the second incident, officers were under gunfire. I responded with lights and sirens, but of course, one of the citizens wasn't paying attention and broad-sided me in an intersection. The car spun around and came to a halt. Out of this, I received a concussion, hurt my back, neck, and knee. Good thing I worked out, because if I didn't, I most likely wouldn't be able to handle the abuse that comes from a car accident. I wouldn't be able to recover as quickly as I did. My point is, when we are driving with our lights and sirens on, get out of the way. Pay attention to what is going on around you.

Now back to my example of the man with the gun; call, and if an officer gets injured responding to the call, I promise you, you will have hell to pay, if that officer is injured or killed responding to your bullshit call. We will track the phone calls down, find out who you are, and lock you up. Then we will sue you for everything you have or don't have. Priority runs are dangerous runs. Don't make up things to get us there faster. I know the people reading this book are like, *I would never do that*. Yeah, right, the people in DC do it every day. Remember, people, we have families too. The world does not revolve around your little problems.

As a police officer, I can tell you most patrol officers don't like the citizens. We tolerate you. We have to be phony just to get along with you. Heaven forbid you get a police officer who isn't so nice on a traffic stop. Your best bet is to do what you are told to do. Bottom line, you don't know what's going on in his head. Just like we don't know what's going on in yours. Do what you're told to do and it will be a pleasant experience. I'll give you some examples. I was driving around on patrol and a dumb white guy stopped me in the middle of the street. He said his lights were off in his house. I told him the lights were out in the area. Now this was the afternoon; he asked, "Could you check other residents' homes and see if their lights are out?" I told him you can't do that. He told me that was my job. I looked at him like he was smoking crack and drove away.

Another time, I responded for a car accident. When I arrived, I spoke with the driver of the one of the vehicles. She told me a car backed into her car and drove off. Now there were other people around, and they started telling me about the skid marks where the other driver sped off. One of the men said, "Look at the skid marks; you should take photos." Then he said, "Do you have a measuring tape to see how long the marks are?" I said, "Sir, thank you for all of your help." I asked him if he witnessed the accident. He said no. I told him he was not helpful for the investigation. He said, "I think you should take photos." I asked him if he knew my job. I told him he could have my gun and badge and do this, since he knew so much. He left abruptly. How is it you citizens know my job better than me? When I get a call at your business or wherever you work, do you ever hear the police telling you how to do your job? No, we don't do that. Stay in your place and don't tell us what to do. When you want to put this uniform on and do this job, feel free to do so.

I was sitting in a restaurant taking my lunch break and this intoxicated lady fell in front of the restaurant. Of course, certain patrons of the restaurant jumped up and were like, "Oh my God, she fell." I was like, *Big deal she fell, who cares?* Now, I was in the middle of eating, and I got up to see if the lady was okay. Before I got to her, she had walked away. Now this black bitch asked me, "Why you didn't do anything?" I asked her, "What did you want me to do?" She asked, "Why you didn't see how she was?" I wanted to respond, *Why didn't you, bitch?* Of course, I kept a professional demeanor and stated to the upset citizen, "She walked away before I could help her." Of course, the black bitch was upset. She started to eye-fuck me; I eye fucked right back. I told her, "We can do this all day long." Then her sorryass black boyfriend just sat there like a woman not saying anything, but smiled at me. I wanted to say to this brotha, *Train your bitch.*

There are also the citizens who like the police, but there are very few in this area. The citizens who like the police will make the officers food. I never eat it. Just because they say they like us doesn't mean it's true. Many restaurants in the area like to have a police presence. Therefore, they will accommodate the police while eating. Many of the people in the DMV have federal jobs they think are important. Well guess what? You're not. At least not to me, I remember this black bitch was parked illegally; I told her she had to move her vehicle. She did. Then she moved her car to another parking place that she was not authorized to park in. I told her she had to move her car again. She became angry and screamed, "I work for the Federal Government! I can't believe the harassment here." Then she got back in her car and said, "I'll never come back here again." I looked at her and said, "Good." I'm thinking to myself, *I hope you don't come back.*

Another time my partner and I were on a traffic stop. During the traffic stop, whitey showed up on the sidewalk. He asked us to move our vehicle. We told him we were busy. He said he wanted to leave. We told him, "Wait." He returned to the restaurant, and then came back out. He said, "I would like to leave." As I told him before, we were busy. Then he pulled out his credentials; he was an inspector from a federal law enforcement agency. He said, "I'm the police too." I said, "If you're the police then why are you interfering with us while we are on this traffic stop?" Then I told him, "Now go away, sir."

After we issued tickets for the violations, I told the inspector to return so I could see his credentials again. I wanted to make sure he wasn't an imposter. He told me he wasn't showing me anything. I told him he had better show me or else he was on his way to jail for impersonating a police officer. I called for an official to the scene. When the official arrived, along with another cruiser, this fed knew he was in trouble. He started to shake and stutter when talking. The inspector showed his credentials and immediately apologized for his behavior. He didn't realize he was on his way to jail. That's the reason I called an official to the scene. We had to take his weapon and notify his supervisor. My sergeant told me not to lock him up. Lucky for him, because I would have ruined him and put his picture and the story in one of our newspapers.

There was this black bitch female DC politician I gave a ticket to. She was parked illegally. When she returned to her vehicle, she asked, "What is this?" I said, "It's a ticket." Then she said, "You obviously don't know how this works." I said, "Yes, ma'am, I do." I said, "You get a ticket and you pay or contest it. That's how this works." She asked for my name. I told her my name and said, "It's also on the ticket."

I was driving and observed a black female talking on her cell phone; she was on the opposite side of the road. Traffic was stopped. I told her put the cell phone down; she told me, "No." I told her, "Put the cell phone down." She told me, "No," again. Then, when the light turned green, she sped off. Of course, I turned my cruiser around and put on my emergency equipment. I chased her down and made my stop. I ran her tag, waited for the return, and made my approach to her vehicle. She was on her cell phone talking to communications telling them to send an official to the location. Many officers arrived, including an official from my district. I asked for her license, registration, and proof of insurance. She then showed me she was a sergeant from my agency. My sergeant at the time pulled me to the side and said, "Don't give her a ticket." He said, "Trust me; she won't forget this incident ever again." I told my sergeant, "Okay. She won't get the ticket." Now when I was late for court one time, she was the sergeant in charge. I told her I was late. She told me, "No you're not. I'll take care of it for you." Guess what? I wasn't late. She pulled me aside. She told me, "The way you came after me in the cruiser, you intimidated me." Then she thanked me for not giving her the ticket. Every time she sees me she always addresses me as: Officer Mac.

What I'm illustrating is the complete arrogance and the inflated egos of people in the DMV. Their self worth isn't all that important. Most important people don't want to make waves. The unimportant people like to make waves because they are unimportant and want to be important.

These are just the last examples I will use. They are about traffic stops and my encounters with males and females—white and black—and the things they say or are thinking. White male: "Why did you stop me? I want to speak with your superior. Do you know who I am?" Then he starts to laugh. This is his arrogance and his ego. Black male: "Is there a problem, officer?" (Thought) *I hope my I don't have any warrants or my license isn't suspended. Oh shit, I hope he doesn't find this crack and gun in my car.* White woman: "Oh hi, officer, is there a problem? Oh I did, thank you for the ticket." Who says thank you for a ticket when the ticket is $500.00 or more? Dumbass white bitches. Black woman: "What? I ain't paying shit. Fuck you, mother fucker." That's the typical black bitch response.

In closing, I would like to say to the citizens, I have a great distain for you. I have no respect for you. You have no respect for yourselves. You're cold and callous, yet you think you are civilized. If you wouldn't help a child in distress, what's that say about you? That's by far one of the lowest things a person can do. You know you are the same as animals, believe it or not. I learned to treat you all the same. I treated you all like some shit, because you deserved it.

Chapter Six

Right is Wrong, Wrong is Right

Welcome to my agency. There is a right way of doing things and there is my agency's way of doing things. This is the land of dysfunction. When I say right is wrong and wrong is right, that's exactly what I mean. Understand that everything is reversed. So when you do work you are wrong. It is expected that you do as little as possible. Most of you would think being in the Washington DC area that law enforcement would be aggressive—the car chases, shootouts, big drug busts, and locking everyone up. Well, it's the complete opposite. This is how this stuff works. This is a political environment. You can't be firm with the citizens. This is the kindler, gentler police department.

What I don't understand is, how can you become gentler when society has become increasingly more violent? It's not going to get any better. The truth with my agency is, they just want you to be visible and be report takers. If you want to be super cop, this is not the agency for that. Believe me, they will terminate or suspend you for a lengthy period of time. This should knock the wind out of your sails. Keep in mind, if you have a house and a family, a termination or suspension can cause a lot of damage to your finances and set your payments back for your mortgage, car note, or your child's education. Just something to think about.

I'll illustrate examples. I remember there was a car chase involving an armed, car-jacked vehicle. A detective from a different district came over the air and said there was a vehicle in our district taken in an armed car-jacking. The officers had eyes on the vehicle. The vehicle was parked. We were waiting for the vehicle to become occupied again. The suspect entered the vehicle. He saw one of the teams and took off. He came straight toward our cruiser and tried to ram my partner and me. My partner got us out of the way as this car missed us. Now we were in pursuit of an armed car-jacked vehicle. Other vehicles joined the pursuit. Now it started to rain, the streets were getting slick, and at some point in time a supervisor got on the air and said, "Cut the chase." Apparently nobody heard him, because they kept chasing. Now this vehicle was trying to lose us. We were driving eastbound; he jumped into the westbound lane, crossed over the median into oncoming traffic, and eventually ran into an area where they were doing construction.

The suspect jumped out of the car and down near a river embankment. The suspect was injured. Well, now he was caught. Come to find out this suspect was wanted on two homicides. The officers who caught this guy were heroes, right? Wrong. After a lengthy investigation, the command staff in all of their infinite knowledge and wisdom decided that this officer disobeyed an order to cut the chase. The captain in charge of the investigation proposed a 20- or 25-day suspension for the officers involved. Now after the appeal process was completed, the officer was given the days, but the officer and the union were going to take the case to the media and embarrass the agency. The union was saying that the agency penalizes officers for apprehending 1) an armed carjacker, and 2) a double homicide suspect. Eventually, the agency backed down and the suspension was rescinded.

This is an incident where an official was working a part-time job. The supervisor was called for an assault inside the location, and the official was told a certain individual committed the assault. The official arrested the suspects and called for an officer to take the arrest. Now the officer, following what the official told him had occurred, took the arrest. This is called: information received. This information is deemed to be credible because it's coming from another police officer. Guess what? The guy who was arrested wasn't involved. The wrongfully accused suspect filed a complaint and it was all downhill from there. Now keep in mind that the officer was getting his information from 1) an official 2) a black bitch. Guess what? Shit was going to be jacked up. Read the chapter: *Bitches in Law Enforcement*, and you will understand further. So my agency proposed a 15-day suspension for this officer for doing his job. Of course, they say shit rolls downhill. My question is and was, *Why didn't you punish the sergeant?* The sergeant has more responsibility than the officer does. It's the sergeant's job to make sure the investigation is complete and thorough; this includes facts, circumstances, and reliable information. If anything, the sergeant should have received a stiffer penalty than the officer. Oh, but not here at this agency; it's the complete opposite.

This example dealt with an officer who was allegedly on the scene of an incident. We came to find out the officer wasn't even working the day the incident occurred. Now during the investigation, all this information was documented. It showed he wasn't working the day of the incident nor was he even in the area. Guess what happened? The agency gave this officer a ten-day suspension. When this officer told me this story, I was in total disbelief. Most people would say he's lying. There has to be something else to this story he's not telling. Well, there isn't. He served the ten days. When it came time for arbitration, of course the arbitrator ruled in his favor and gave his money and his days back. So it was like a paid vacation. But the officer had to wait one year for the arbitration process.

Understand this job is only 10 to 15 percent physical; it is 85 to 90 percent mental. That's why you have to be mentally strong when dealing with this agency, because you can actually lose your mind with the things this agency does to its officers and officials. An officer once told me, "If you were not a psycho before you took the job, you will be once they get done with you." I was once asked, "What does it mean when you fail the psychological?" My response was, "You're not fucked up enough for the job." This means you have to deal with so many challenging situations that you need to be mentally strong to deal with them. The things the agency does to you can actually cause severe stress. The stress of this job and outside factors play heavily on an officer's mental and physical health. Many young officers die from heart attacks, strokes, and other ailments. Stress can manifest itself in many ways.

I'll give you examples of what I'm talking about. There was an official who went to a district in his PJs and used a marked departmental vehicle. This official was driving around and went to a club and wanted to arrest people. The official was transported to a mental health clinic and committed for observation. This official was eventually promoted. There was another official who was caught running down the street with his eight-point hat on and a pistol belt and nothing more. I know people are saying, "There is no way." Well, people, there is a way. This is normal for this agency.

Racism and the community: Here's a topic that will cause some discussion. As many people know, DC was at one point the murder capitol of the United States. This was in the late 1980's and the early '90s. It is now the fourth most violent city in the United States. Most of the violence is niggaz on niggaz, but every once in a while, the niggaz will kill some dumbass whitey or seriously hurt him. When the death or serious bodily injury is caused by some niggaz to whitey, you can best believe the department will be out in full force. The department will spend all kinds of over-time money to make whitey feel safe. Also, best believe the agency will apprehend the individuals responsible for their acts of violence perpetrated to the most precious and valuable resource—the white woman. The truth is, a black person's life is not as valuable as a white person's life. Many of you would disagree with me. I don't know why. It's the truth. I will show examples of how this works.

Back in the early or mid 2000's, there was a white couple robbed and killed in a very violent manner. When this occurred, everyone in the department was working overtime. We were out every night for an additional four hours. All of this to show whitey he is secure. The best part about this is they caught those savages in a timely manner. In the same time frame, there were numerous young black males killed by unknown niggaz. Keep in mind the black males had no known drug affiliation or gang affiliation; these were good students in school. Most of them were at the wrong place at the wrong time. If there is any such thing now, why isn't the same applied? There was no over-time; the department was not out in full force. A death is not always a death. It is dependent upon the circumstances. An innocent life taken is just that. They deserve the same respect. Now if they are pieces of shit, then it's a totally different story. I'm talking about drug dealers, gang members, thugs, and everyone else who falls within that category.

Recently, there was a rash of robberies of white women in the area. Many of these white women were seriously injured. You know what happened? That's right, send in the cavalry. There was a strong police presence in the neighborhood. On every corner there was a police car along with officers on foot. Now as I stated earlier in my chapter: *Dumbass Whitey*, these white women put themselves in situations that they don't need to be in. For example, they just walk aimlessly in front of low-income housing that usually has bars around the entire complex. Now if I was walking and saw this, I would say to myself, *there are bars around this* complex, *which must mean there are wild animals inside.* Then I would walk far away from that complex because it is a safety issue. In contrast, if the same thing were to happen to black people, the department would never enforce the amount of resources they used for these Dumbasss Whiteys. Of course we are in a recession, so there really is no over-time.

Now, I know many of you reading this are going to say, "He's fucked up," but here it is. Many times we would hope for one of those niggaz to go on a rampage killing or severely injuring whitey so we could get some over-time money. As I said in the chapters on *Niggaz*, Niggaz create job security. One time in roll call a white officer said, "Kill a cracka and get all the over-time you want." Once again, I say that the life of a whitey is more valuable than black persons. I will also say a white person will get preferential treatment over any other group. I will give more examples. For instance citizen complaints.

Most citizen complaints happen when officers write tickets for traffic infractions. I'm speaking from experience. I used to write so many traffic tickets. Matter of fact, I used to be the traffic car for my section. Then I started to get complaints. The majority of the complainants said I was rude; they didn't like my tone or my demeanor. The area I worked in was mixed, but there were more whites than blacks. When whites complained about getting tickets, I was brought into my lieutenant's office. He and I had a conversation about treatment of whitey. He said, "Don't you think you should treat a certain group differently than another group?" I told him, "No. I treat everyone the same. There is no preferential treatment for anyone." Then he stated, "You can't treat everyone the same." I responded, "I beg to differ."

I believe in being consistent. If the white person did something, he gets a ticket. If the black person did something, he gets a ticket. If the old man did something, he gets a ticket. If the old woman did something, she gets a ticket. Bottom line is consistency. If you're not consistent, this can lead to problems for you as an officer. Problems of discrimination and/or harassment if a complaint is filed. Furthermore, when those tickets are filed, they can find out the sex and race of the driver. The last thing an officer wants to do is answer why he or she was giving one group of people tickets and not the other. Keep in mind; I used to investigate police misconduct. I'm very well aware of things that will get an officer in trouble. You know what I do now? I don't write tickets. This way there are no complaints. An officer once told me, "If you don't do shit, can't nobody say shit." Bottom line, in a discrete way my lieutenant was telling me to stop doing my job. Now in the same discussion he said, "If the complaints came from an area with a bunch of niggaz, the complaints wouldn't be taken seriously." I'm thinking to myself, *What the fuck kind of bullshit is this?*

Another time my lieutenant called me into his office; this meeting had to deal with me not being nice to whitey. White people would complain and say I was mean and didn't smile. I was instructed to smile by this lieutenant. My response to him was, "You smile at them. That's your job. I'm not the white folk's nigger. Maybe you are, but I'm not." Then I said to him, "You want me to tap dance and sing Mammie too, Boss Sir?" He then asked, "Why can't you be nice?" My response was, "Being nice on the street will get you killed, even by whitey." He said to me, "Get the fuck out of my office." I responded by saying, "Yaz sir, mister Boss Sir." Then I started thinking to myself, *I could get into some trouble because of my behavior*. Then I thought, *He doesn't like to write. He has enough work to do. I'm safe.*

The point I'm making is that in law enforcement you must remain consistent. It's like this: either you treat all people good or you treat them all like shit. I prefer the second. If you treat them the same, there is no wiggle room when the outside agencies want to investigate the department on issues of disparity.

Politics and law enforcement: I really don't think politics and law enforcement should intertwine. Politics is politics and law enforcement is law enforcement. The mayor's office, city council, or the department should not show favoritism toward citizens or the police. Their stands should be neutral. If you are from any elected office, never come out after an incident occurs and say the police were wrong. Let the facts show if the police were wrong in their actions. It's hard enough when the citizens aren't fans of yours. Then you tell them the police were wrong even before an investigation has started and has been completed. If you want the police to do their jobs and do them well, then it's best to keep your mouth shut. Also, the citizens should have very little impact on what decisions are made within the agency. I know community-oriented policing is good, but at the same time it can be detrimental when the citizens have such a strong influence on what occurs. Best believe the agency will throw you under the bus if any negative publicity comes out. Cops would say, *It's time to send some meat to the altar. There's going to be a sacrifice.* As I said in the beginning, you can be 100 percent correct and still be wrong. I will show examples.

There was on officer who was involved in a shooting with some niggaz. Two officers shot and killed a nigga; the kid had a gun and fired at the officers. The officers returned fire, striking the assailant. But one of the animals moved the gun from the scene. This made it seem as if the officers shot and killed unarmed black youth. This was far from the truth. Now, someone from a political office at the time came out and said the police were wrong. The city even paid for the funeral for the youth, even though he was wrong. At the same time, those officers were being smashed, and their reputations were being questioned. It took some time to sort out. But when the weapon used in the officer's shooting was used in another shooting, the weapon was recovered, and the ballistics matched. This sheds a whole new light on the situation. Now what does that political officer have to say?

This is something that happened to me. There was an ANC commissioner (Advisory Neighborhood Commission) in our area who was no good. These commissioners are powerless, but for some reason she knew the Chief of Police at the time. She had an arrest record and was known to file frivolous police reports. Now keep in mind this was a real black bitch. There was a time when we had to attend community meetings and she would be there. She would bring food and other items. When my partner and I arrived at the meeting, she was waiting outside with the food. She told me, "Pick that stuff up and take it into the meeting." Oh my dear, you obviously don't know who you are speaking with. I told her to, "Pick it up yourself, and you carry it in." Well, guess what? It's game on. My partner stepped in and said, "I'll take the stuff." It was like I challenged her authority. She had none.

Another time, an officer made traffic stop of this commissioner. The officer called for an additional unit. It just happened to be me who assisted the officer. When I arrived, I was like, *Great, now I'm involved in this bullshit too*. This black bitch refused to give the officer any of her information. Then she called the watch commander for assistance. The watch commander told her, "You better comply with the officer's request." After he said that, she did. She was really pissed at me. She asked me, "Why you didn't help me?" I told her, "I didn't stop you. It's not my place." The officer gave her two tickets. Then came the complaint, which wasn't even a complaint. The complaint was investigated and I never heard about it again. Now this big black bitch had an ego the size of Texas and thought her shit didn't stink. But here is the kicker. This is some crud ball shit.

We were working a special attention in the area of this lady's house. She called the police several times during the day saying there were children playing in front of her house. Of course we responded and did our little dance for this black bitch. Then she called back a few hours later saying the kids had threatened her, and ran over her flowers on their bike. When I arrived, I observed the flowers were pulled out from the ground. This is inconsistent with someone running over flowers on a bike. There were children outside and some teenagers. She said she wanted the kids off of the street. I told her just as long as they were not on her property but on the street there was nothing I could do.

She went into her house to get a camera and started taking pictures of the youths outside. The kids were laughing at her, because she was an idiot. She called the district and asked for another car to come. She said I wasn't helpful to her. When the other officer arrived they asked her what happened. She explained that some of the children were in front of her house and she didn't want them there. The officers asked her if she had been threatened that night. She said, "No." Furthermore, an official arrived on the scene and he was now in charge. At no time did she say she was threatened by anyone to the official. Now I was on leave when she filed a report and a citizen complaint stating I was on the scene when she was threatened and I didn't do anything. Now, once this shit hit the commander's desk, she told an official to take a report and lock up the individual responsible for the alleged threats. The officers did what theofficial told them to do. Now keep in mind there was no investigation, only her word. The officers got an arrest warrant and locked up the kid for nothing.

When I came back off of leave, I was called to the captain's office. He told me I was being placed on non-contact (non-contact is when they take your credentials and your department-issued Glock 19 or 17, and you have no police powers) until this investigation was completed. I was like, *Really? Are you really being serious?*

When the US Attorney got the case, this black bitch and her daughter were called down to the grand jury. I wanted them to testify, but it didn't get that far. If she testified, it would have been the nail in her coffin. I was the target of a criminal investigation. The complaint was sent to the United States Attorney's office for criminal prosecution; the charge was failure to take police action. When the US Attorney declined to prosecute, the administrative charge became: neglect of duty. They actually thought of terminating me. Then they changed my discipline to 25 days, which was ridiculous. Now during the investigation, it showed this bitch filed a false police report and also made false statements. She caused all this damage. Do you think anything happened to her? Hell no. Now the official conducting the investigation sent the paperwork to another law enforcement agency for them to investigate, because she was in bed with the ANC bitch. This way if something happened to the ANC broad, the lieutenant, who was also another black bitch, could say, "I didn't lock you up." It's called recusing yourself from the investigation. Bottom line, if they would have attempted to terminate me and succeeded, best believe you would have heard about this incident, because everyone who was involved knew I was coming for them.

As I said earlier, violence is a behavior modification tool. When used appropriately, it works. Now, after working hard to get where you have to get in life, then to see it almost come crashing down in front of your face can truly piss you off, especially over some bullshit. This incident could have severely ruined my life for future employment and other issues. I see it like this, if *I* don't have then *you* won't have. If I can't eat then you won't eat. If I suffer then you will suffer too. It's that simple. Perhaps people will think twice before they do some dumb shit. Well, it turned out good for me; they recommended a 25-day suspension and I never served a day. The bad part about this was I was about to be hired as a federal agent. When they found out I was on non-contact, they couldn't even touch me.

One must understand that law enforcement is a business; this is how they may get you to quit. Think about this, if an officer does 25 years on the job and retires as a sergeant, most likely he will get between 60,000 and 70,000 dollars a year for the rest of his life, plus his medical benefits will be paid. The flip side of that is if they can get rid of as many officers through quitting, being fired, or through death. Who do you think benefits? The government does. They don't have to pay out that money. Keep in mind, everything revolves around economics, even law enforcement. In closing out this chapter, I will say you can be 100 percent correct in everything you did in your police actions, including professionalism, but when a complaint is filed and investigated, we can still be wrong.

Chapter Seven
Less is More

This chapter is dedicated to the hard-working officers who have lost their jobs just for doing their jobs. This chapter discusses what happens when a cop goes above and beyond his job. First, less is more is also known as "doing the minimum maximum." This means you do what you are required to do and no more. As I have said in the previous chapters, you can actually get suspended or lose your job by doing your job. All you have to do is to accumulate numerous complaints. Regardless of the outcomes of the complaints, the agency can proceed with termination. For example, I had four investigations going on at one time. They were all adverse actions. Actually, none of the four were even close to rising to the level of adverse action.

When they are tired of you, they will up a recommendation. Maybe the recommendation is for an official reprimand; they will change it to adverse action. Maybe the recommendation is for a letter of prejudice, and they change it to adverse action. What I'm saying is, if they are tired of you they will find a way to get rid of you. Even if it doesn't rise to the level. In my agency, you get four adverse actions and they will put you up for termination.

Even if it is investigated and you are cleared. They are looking for a pattern. The agency can come back and still give you days.

For example, my partner and I received a report of a burglary. When we arrived on the scene, we interviewed the complainant and she said she wanted to file a police report in the morning. The reason she wanted to do this was because she was tired and wanted to go home. Furthermore, the complainant had closed the gate to the establishment. The complainant said she also found a driver's license inside of the establishment. Keep in mind this is a warehouse where food is sold. The next morning an officer was dispatched to the warehouse for the burglary. When the officer found out we were on the scene the day before he said, "We should have taken a police report." When the detective arrived, he obtained statements. One of the statements was from an individual who was not there on the scene. According to his statement, he said he gave identification to my partner and me. Later, during the investigation, a gun was found inside of the establishment. Of course, they accused us of not doing our jobs. They went to the length of making this an adverse action. Instead of calling us in and asking us what happened, they just wrote up a notice of proposed adverse action—failure to take a police report. The agency actually made this a criminal charge and sent this to the United States Attorney's Office for criminal prosecution.

First of all, this isn't even criminal in nature. This is an administrative investigation. The funny thing about it is when the detective said the male was on the scene and he wasn't. I obtained a statement from the store manager. The female made it perfectly clear that the male wasn't even there when my partner and I were on scene. The reason I knew to talk with the owner was that she was the one we spoke with. I obtained a statement from her. This way the agency could not write whatever they wanted to write in the investigative report. I blocked whatever they attempted to do. My partner and I would have had no recourse if I had not obtained a statement from the witness. Then the agency said I interfered with the investigation. Keep in mind, I had a right to a defense. That is a constitutional right. I know, sure as hell, they didn't have my best interest in hand. Then they charged me with some violation of the general order that didn't even apply to what I did. During the lieutenant's investigation, it came back that there was no misconduct. This was sent up the chain. Guess what? The assistant chief didn't like the outcome and ordered the lieutenant to give both of us days. Fifteen days for him and twenty-five for me. I'm like, *What the fuck? This is how you conduct business?* Now I'm really pissed. I called my attorney. He told me to just wait and let the union handle it. We went through the appeal process. They violated all the contractual regulations. Then they said for us to start serving the days. My partner served his, I served mine. After this was over, my partner's case went to arbitration. He won his case. My case didn't even make it to arbitration. The agency settled with me. They just gave me my money and my days back. It took about a year for this to happen, but that's how it goes around there. So from that point on, I made sure to do as little as possible. I just answered the radio and nothing more. All you have to do is kick me in the ass one time, and I think that is enough.

So when I say cops do the minimum maximum, there is a reason for that. Many more cops have been through worse than that. It's ridiculous for an officer to have to put up with that type of bullshit. This is why officers do the minimum to help people, because this is a thankless job. This is why officers don't like citizen interaction, because sometimes it can be your last interaction. Most officers have the mentality of: fuck this place and this job. Many officers know after about five to ten years on the job that this job is some bullshit. All of the aggressiveness has left, now you're just a cop who doesn't want to do anything. That's because you have seen the system at work. I know of an officer who worked in narcotics and closed out a couple of homicides. He didn't show up for a few witness conferences at the US Attorney's office and they attempted to terminate him. They didn't terminate him, but he vowed to never do shit for this agency again. Many officers have left the agency after this kind of shit. Trust me, after working for this agency, you will get a job working in law enforcement anywhere.

The hard-working police officer is a fool. You can make all of the arrests in the world, but as soon as you mess up, they forget the good. All the agency remembers is the bad. That's why after getting burned by the agency, cops do nothing. When I say nothing, I mean nothing. Sometimes officers won't even answer the radio and won't go to assignments. That's pretty sad. This is what people don't see. What goes on inside of a police department.

Chapter Eight

Bitches in Law Enforcement

As you can see, this chapter is going to cause some bitches to be upset. I think some women are about to be in their feelings. Before I start, I would like to say that prior to working in law enforcement; these bitches weren't shit to begin with. Now they have some authority and they go crazy. Now remember what I told you about black bitches in the other section of the book. Well, it just carries over to this job. As I stated, most of these women weren't shit before they took this job; now look at them. They know everything; good luck telling them something, because they won't listen. They screw everything up. Remember what I said about bitches lacking reasoning skills; well here it is. As a police officer, you have to be logical and analytical. These bitches are emotional in how they think. They let their emotions guide what they do. So expect some jacked up things to happen when dealing with women in law enforcement. Now, I've had some female partners in the past. This is how I know. All of them were black. I will share some of my experiences with you. This way you can see how I arrive at my conclusion.

This is one female officer who should have never been a police officer. This woman is the worst. I mean the worst. No sense of logic. Everything for her is: *I feel this is wrong*. Forget what the law says. I remember I had to work with her one day. This is a day I will never forget. We were assigned to a hospital detail for someone who had some charge. When we got in the cruiser, she told me she would drive. I had no problem with that. Well, bad idea. She didn't know how to get to the hospital. I was like, *You're driving and you don't know how to get there?* While we were driving she attempted to put us into service. She had the mic in one had and was trying to steer with the other. What was funny is that when she would turn the steering wheel she would have to use both hands, because she wasn't coordinated enough to use the steering wheel and use the mic at the same time. She would have to put the mic down every time we would turn. I told her, "You suck." I asked what her background was. She said she graduated from a university in DC. Then she wanted to attend law school.

When we arrived at the hospital, we went to the room and relieved the other officers and handcuffed the prisoner. We sat there for seven hours watching the prisoner. For seven hours, I had to hear her mouth. I asked her, "Don't you ever shut up?" She asked me why I was so mean to her. I told her she was an idiot, and that was the way I treated idiots. Now when we were leaving, there were some hucks parked in a "no parking zone" behind our cruiser. I asked them why they were parked behind our cruiser, and they said they were waiting for someone. I asked the driver for ID. I told him to move the vehicle because they were illegally parked. Now keep in mind there were four hucks in this SUV. Smoked out windows and when they put the windows down, here are the do-rags, cornrows, and sunglasses at night. I was like, *It figures*. Then she wanted to know what was going on. She said I should tell her what was going on. I was like, *Why? You're useless*. Then I told her about the hucks. She said I shouldn't call them hucks and the reason I did call them hucks was because they were black. I'm like, *Are you serious? Are you a cop or are you some super liberal?* She really became angry then. I told her, "Give me the car keys. As long as I have to ride with you, you will never drive." As we were riding back to the district, she said I was an asshole. I said, "Thanks for the compliment." I asked her, "Why did you become a police officer?" She didn't respond. I told her again, "You suck." She was almost in tears by this point. I'm laughing. She said she never wanted to ride with me again. I was like, *Good*. I was about to drop her ass off on the Southeast /Southwest Freeway. If I had done that, I would have caused many problems for myself. I tried my best to help this bitch by giving her advice, answering her questions, showing her through examples, etc., but she still did the same dumbass shit. It's as if she was stuck on stupid.

As time went on, we never got along. She would say hi to me, and I would say nothing to her. She would ask me, "Why are you so mean to me?" I would respond, "Because you're an idiot." There was one incident where we had to respond to a radio run. When we both arrived on scene, I went over to her cruiser to ask her what happened. She said, "It was nothing." As I was on the passenger's side of the car with my head inside talking to her, she intentionally put the car in reverse, and hit the accelerator in an attempt to run my feet over. Of course, I was quick enough to get out of the way. She tilted her head back and started to laugh. I guess she was somewhat angry because of my alleged mistreatment of her. I know the majority of her peers didn't and don't think highly of this female officer, because she is not police material. I could see her and a civil rights activist walking hand in hand, protesting something the police had done. This female is emotional and has no reasoning skills.

I remember one time in roll call, we were discussing a police shooting and the aftermath of the shooting. The one male officer had his facts in order and gave a half-way decent presentation of what occurred. Then here comes this dummy. She said when she was in college she was involved in plays about the incident. I was like, *Are you serious? Plays? What is wrong with you?* I said to her she couldn't even articulate any of the facts. She said I was a jerk. I told her she was by far the dumbest female police officer I had ever met. But the funniest thing about this is, she was promoted to sergeant. Now, this is how it normally works. The officers who are garbage as officers get promoted and are even worse as officials. When you have less than five years on the job, you really don't know the job, especially if you don't come from an aggressive district. The best officials—male and female—were good or great officers. They have good interpersonal skills and can relate to their subordinates and the public at the same time. This black female official, from what I've heard from people at her current district, is some garbage. No one respected her. I'm sure you can see why.

The other black officer grew up in an area in which I patrolled. This was the hood. You know the saying: you can take the girl out of the hood, but you can't take the hood out of the girl. She was ghetto as hell. Loud as can be. I was like, *Damn. I can't get away from these ghetto bitches on this job*. She worked narcotics for a while and was pretty good at it. I wonder why. I remember when I had to ride with her in the winter; it would be really cold outside. I would put down my window all the way. She would tell me put my window up, because she was cold. I kept my window down hoping she would freeze and get out of the car. I hated riding with her. When the sergeant would give us our assignment he would say the call sign, my name, and her name. I would say, "Sergeant, please change my assignment." I told him, "We do not get along."

Not too long ago, this officer's house was raided by a federal law enforcement agency. The reason was they were looking something . Her boyfriend was allegedly a drug dealer. I'm sure that federal law enforcement agency was watching her for some time. She always told me she would always have more money than me, and then smirk in my face. Furthermore, she would come to work in this highly expensive car. If it was a used model, fine. If not, where are you getting money like that? I'm so glad she is a person of high moral character and has a good value system. It put such a good name on our agency.

But this is the DMV. The majority of the women on the department are ghetto. They think because they have a decent-paying job now, they are not ghetto. Do you know how many instances we have had of these black bitches assisting drug dealers, or having them as their boyfriends? It's pretty sad.

Like most women officers, she didn't want to do anything. I wouldn't want her for assistance if anything happened. You would be fighting by yourself. That's what happens when most women are on the scene and something happens.

This happened recently as well. Matter of fact, it made the paper. There was an officer who went out to eat with his wife and other family members. The off-duty officer went to the restroom, and a woman took his seat. When the officer returned, he asked the female to move. The female moved and then her friends started throwing epithets at the off-duty officer's table. The female who got up grabbed a bottle and shattered the glass on the officer's wife's face. The wife was knocked to the floor, and the female continued to slash the wife's face, according to the police report. The officer removed the attacker from his wife. His wife received more than 100 stitches in her face.

A black female watch commander arrived and told the officer, "You need to respond to the station and complete paperwork." The officer said, "My wife is going to the emergency room; the administrative paperwork can wait." The black female watch commander allegedly told the officer, "If you value your job, you will do what I told you to do." The officer was in his personal vehicle, and the lieutenant and a sergeant allegedly forced him to leave his car and ride in a cruiser to the station to complete three hours worth of paperwork. His wife was in the hospital. Do you think the watch commander offered to take him to see his wife? Of course not. Did the bitch ask how his wife was doing? Nope. But this is typical of these black bitches in law enforcement. They are the worst at making decisions; everything with them has to do with their authority. No logic, just, *I'm in charge*. Any normal person would have said, "Complete the paperwork later. You need to be with your wife." Now keep in mind, I said a normal person.

I had a female official from day one who I knew was going to be a problem. I remember I submitted a training request for her to initial and be sent up in the chain of command. When I approached her, she looked at the request and said, "This isn't a good idea." I asked her why it wasn't. She couldn't even give a valid response. She failed to initial the document. I found another sergeant from my area, and he initialed the paperwork and sent it through the proper channels. I was informed by other officers from the district where she used to work, and how she was worthless as an officer. I was told she never went into service and when she did go into service she would not answer the radio. I was also told to stay away from her and not to trust her. Now this black bitch sergeant wasn't popular with the majority of the officers. Many officers went to the commander and asked to be moved to another part of the district where they wouldn't have any contact with this sergeant.

I remember one day she wanted to see me about a citizen complaint. She told me to write a statement about the incident.

I asked her if this was criminal or administrative. She told me to just write a statement. I told her unless she told me if it was criminal or not, I wasn't writing anything. Then she copped an attitude and threw the complaint on the desk in my direction. I asked her, "Who you think you are?" I told her, "You tell us to respect the citizens and treat them kindly, but you can't even treat your subordinates with respect." Furthermore, I told her, "I'm not your child or your man. You will not address me in that manner or that tone, do I make myself clear?" Then she told me to leave the roll call room and go downstairs. About 30 minutes later, she came downstairs and told me to write a statement about the incident. She said that the investigation was administrative in nature. I'm saying this, all of this, could have been avoided if she would have told me from the beginning what the nature of the complaint was. Approximately five months later, she was promoted and left the district. My lieutenant told me he had something for me. He gave me the so-called discipline, in reference to the story above. I told him this happened five months ago, and asked why she didn't (my official at that time) give this to me when it happened. He took the discipline back and disposed of it.

There was an incident when a vehicle accident occurred on private property, I took the report for the accident and submitted the report to the black bitch female sergeant. She asked why I took the report. I explained to her the circumstances and the general order pertaining to accidents on private property. She said she didn't like the answer and refused to sign it. I asked her, "What is your problem?" Two other officials in the room said, "Mac, get it signed later." I found another official and he signed it with no hesitation. Now my question is, what is your reasoning for not signing the paperwork? Most of the time, these supervisors will do things because they can. This is just an example of how not to be as supervisor.

Another incident with the same black bitch sergeant happened when she backed up another officer on a traffic stop. I obviously was doing something else while the officer was on the stop. Her complaint was that I was in the same block as the officer and didn't assist him. So she attempted to discipline me with paperwork. Of course, I violated no general order, but she decided to write me up anyway. When she and another official attempted to give me the so-called discipline, I read it and laughed in her face. I told her, "The facts are wrong." She had the wrong dates, wrong locations. I told her and the other sergeant, "Take this back." She then called in the officer who was on the stop to interview him. He told her she was incorrect with the facts. I heard nothing else about it. Instead of asking me what happened, she just started writing. If she would have known the circumstances and facts behind what had occurred, she could have saved herself a lot of keystrokes on the computer. This is what I mean about bitches lacking reasoning skills.

At times, we were allowed to choose the area in which we wanted to work. This black bitch sergeant picked a certain area. When it came time for the officers to pick where they wanted to work and they saw her name, the slots were empty. I think officers filled two or three slots. Most officers would want to work in that area. But when they saw who the sergeant was, everyone picked another area. Even the officers who were in that area left when they saw she was the sergeant. I think the officers' selections speak volumes. This incident is with the same black bitch official . We were in roll call and she (the official) was giving out assignments. We were short on manpower and she decided to place me in the station. Now anybody who has worked with me knows better than to put me in the station because I would have to deal with the citizens. When I asked her to "reassign me," she said, "Take your assignment." I said, "Okay." I went to the station and started to feel ill. I informed her that I wasn't "feeling well." Now our policy says that if you don't feel well, notify an official and respond to the clinic, which I did. The clinic sent me home and gave me three days off. You see, if you had just sent someone else to the station to work, then you wouldn't have had this problem. Keep in mind we were already short on manpower; now you're down one more person. I just gave her the big "Fuck You." Needless to say, I was never assigned to the station again.

I was in a cruiser and it was close to check-off. The alert tone sounded and there was a 10-50 with injuries. (That is a car accident with injuries.) I received the assignment but it wasn't in my area of patrol. When I arrived, this lady had jumped a curb and run into a fence near a stadium. I'm stuck there waiting for the ambulance and other personnel to extract this woman from her vehicle. Then I had to go to the hospital to check on her condition and obtain a statement from her. This is a time-consuming process. After that, I still had to do the accident report. When it was time for check-off, I told the check-off official to "box me in;" that means hold me over until I finish and arrest or accident. The check-off official was the black bitch . When I responded back to the station I told her what had occurred. She told me I had ten minutes to finish the accident report. I looked at her and said, "Okay." The computer program for the 10-50 wasn't working properly, which meant I had to do the report by hand. This takes forever to do. When I was doing the report she told me if I didn't finish shortly, I wasn't going to get paid. I just looked at her. I waited for the black bitch to leave and asked the midnight roll call official if it was okay for me to work a continuation of my tour because of the paperwork involved. I wouldn't have to work the following day. The midnight roll call official said, "Okay," but he had to ask the watch commander for midnights; the watch commander said yes.

So I worked 16 hours straight, and I didn't have to report back to work for my tour of duty, which was 2:00 p.m. until 10:30 p.m. The funny thing about this was they were short on manpower during evening tour. When I didn't show up for work, they called me at my residence and asked, "Why are you not here?" I explained to them that I worked midnights and I didn't have to come to work because midnights were my tour of duty for the day. The roll call official said, "We are short on man power." I responded, "That's your problem," and hung up the phone. The point I'm making here is if you want to play "fuck fuck," then let's play. The best part about all of this is I wasn't working with a bunch of rocket scientists. Especially when it came to this black bitch. Ever since that incident occurred, she has looked at me like, *You fucking snake.* Well, truth be told, I looked at her like that from day one. I just gave her another, "Fuck you, bitch." A black bitch female lieutenant from a different district was in my district getting something to eat when a citizen said a man had a knife and pulled it out on him. Of course the citizen didn't stay around, but the lieutenant made the stop of the individual who allegedly had a knife. I was flagged down by this lieutenant and she told me what had occurred. I asked how long ago this happened. She told me, "About five minutes ago." I asked, "Where's the complainant, and did you pat the individual down to see if he had the knife?" She told me that was my job. I said, "You stopped him. Did you pat him down for officer safety?" She asked, "Are you questioning me?" I said, "Yes, I am." Then I asked her again, "Did you pat him down?" Then she really got pissed. Then, like the typical ghetto bitch she is, she started rolling her neck, hands on her hips, and she told me, "I am a lieutenant," at the same time I'm patting this guy down for the knife. He didn't have one on him. Now I asked the lieutenant, "Where is the complainant?" She had no response. Then she asked for my name and badge. I asked the same of her. She called one of my sergeants to the scene and my sergeant had to hear her rant and rave about the incident.

Bottom line, the majority of these black bitches in supervisory positions really don't need to be there. It's truly a shame because there is such a lack of professionalism with these black bitches. I've had two great black female supervisors the entire time I've been with my agency. Not only were they good supervisors, they were great people. I liked them and I respected them. One of them retired and the other was transferred to another division. I miss them dearly. I can truly say this about the both of them; I wish they were still here and were my supervisors. The rest of these black bitch supervisors I wouldn't piss on if they were on fire.

There are some important things to realize. The majority of these women don't have very much education. If they were not doing this job, I believe they would be sitting on a stool somewhere, swiping credit cards and telling people how much their meals cost. Perhaps they might be with a drug dealer or be dancing around a pole at a strip club.

White bitches: Now I have worked with a few of these white women. There are some similarities between black and white women. For example, they don't listen, and they think they know more than you do. I just sit back and watch them mess something up. Then they want your assistance. I tell them, "You got yourself into this, now let's see you get yourself out." But I will say this about the white females: they are somewhat more professional than the black women. They speak better English. They are not loud and know when to keep their mouths shut. For the most part, you can ask them a question without getting a bunch of attitude. As far as dealing with white female supervisors, I have not had the opportunity to do so. The one occasion I dealt with one of them, she was professional. Not only that, but I have known her since we were in the academy together.

Chapter Nine

The Boy in Blue Will Fuck You Too (Management)

My agency was notorious for doing things that made no sense. I blame this on their lack of management training and conducting business as if this was customer service as opposed to a law enforcement organization. If the training they are receiving deals with a customer service approach, then we as officers should be given a notepad; and after every citizen encounter they should be asked to fill out a survey on how the service was. Actually, we already have this form. It is used on a regular basis. It's pretty sad that a police department of this size is concerned about what the citizens say. How does an agency like this allow the citizens to have such an influence on what occurs? People should know that perception is reality, but in all honesty it isn't. Perception is not reality; many things in law enforcement are all smoke and mirrors.

At the line supervisor level, there needs to be more training on how to manage people. Also, on decision-making skills. I can say this: some of the male supervisors made or can make good, logical decisions. As a line supervisor, you are there to back up your people on the street. Most times they will do that or diffuse a situation that could be potentially detrimental to an officer (citizen complaints). Most female line supervisors once again are emotional and lack reasoning skills. Another thing I have noticed is sometimes outcomes of an investigation are based upon if they like you or not. Many times this agency will slant the investigation based on political reasons. If something looks bad in the media, it doesn't matter how right the officer is, he will be thrown under the bus. All to save face. I blame management for caving into what the public wants. When you as an agency train us and we follow how we were trained and the general orders, it doesn't matter what you think or how you would have done something. All that matters is he didn't violate a general order or the law. These investigations are supposed to be fact-finding. These are objective—rather than subjective—investigations. I will give you two examples.

I was called for a car accident. The woman who called, called from her residence. The accident happened at another location. When I spoke with this lady she told me the bicycle officers told her she could get an accident report if she called. I told the lady that was incorrect. When the other person left her information on this woman's windshield she now had the other party's information. All she had to do was to go to the woman's house and confirm who she was and her insurance information. Just to make sure the information was correct; I called the lady who struck her car. She told me what happened and I asked her if I could meet with her to exchange insurance and other information. The woman had no problems. Now the woman who was the complainant was so angry because she couldn't get a police report that she went to file a complaint on me.

When the lady filed this complaint, of course I had to give a statement about why I didn't write a report for this woman. Of course, the charge was neglect of duty, failure to file a police report. After I explained to this dumb white bitch our policy and procedure about minor car accidents, she still wanted a report. I can't understand why this agency entertains these simple ass people. Please refer to *Dumbass Whitey* in reference to the complaint and the individual who filed it. As I said about whitey in the chapter, they whine, bitch, and moan when they can't get their way. Bottom line, the results proved I didn't do anything wrong, but they said I interfered in the investigation because I found a witness to counter what the white bitch who filed the complaint said. When the investigation was completed, the lieutenant told me he had to give me the discipline. Yet it had no general order I violated. I asked him, "What's the general order I violated?" He said, "I'm sure there is one, but we can't find it." I just laughed. I said, "Whatever." This is how management works in my agency.

It was time for check-off, and I was returning to the district. There was a vehicle stopped in the street. As I pulled in to park, I asked her to pull up over the loudspeaker; she did and I fit my cruiser in the space. Now keep in mind, there was another space for her to park right in front of me. As I turned off the cruiser and gathered my belongings, a lady exited her vehicle and said, "That's my parking space." I looked at her and kept walking to the station and responded for check-off. Of course, she filed a complaint. She alleged I abused my police powers because I took "her" parking space, as if she owned it. Refer to *Dumbass Whitey*.

When I gave my statement, I violated no general order. Of course they said I should have given up the space for the dumb white bitch just for community relations. I was like, *Really? Since when did this become a general order?* Also, I asked what general order this was, because they didn't have one listed. I asked for a commander's conference. At the commander's conference, it was an inspector who did the proceeding. I was there with my union rep. The inspector was a black bitch; she asked me if I understood what I did was wrong. I said, "No, why don't you explain it to me?" She said, "You were wrong." I asked, "What general order did I violate?" She asked, "You don't understand how you were wrong and attempted to intimidate me?" at the same time by her posturing and her voice inflections. I said, "Nope." She said, "You get the discipline." I just laughed. Because I didn't cave in to what she wanted me to cave in to. Now keep in mind, I didn't violate any general order but they still gave me discipline. Remember, I worked police misconduct. I know what they are allowed to do and how the investigations are to be completed. In reference to this inspector, read the chapter: *Bitches in Law Enforcement*. I appealed the decision and never heard about the discipline again. My union rep told me, "I'm glad you didn't cave in."

I have said before that in the past I have had good officials and bad ones. I'll show you from the commanders down what my officials were like. At my first district, I had a black bitch as a commander. She was heavy-set and very unprofessional. One day I was outside of her office listening to how she spoke to some of the captains and lieutenants. She said, "Look, you dumb mutha fuckers, I need this shit to be done now." The one female lieutenant (another hood rat) told her, "Who do you think you are talking to, you fat bitch?" I'm outside of her office listening to all of this, and the captain, who was a black male, was just laughing at the entire situation. I'm like, *Shit, she talks to people like that, and that's so unprofessional*. But that is to be expected here. They are typical. Furthermore, the district represents the commander. So if the district is messed up, then it's a reflection of the commander. This district was a mess.

The captain, a black male, had an accident one evening and asked for additional units. We, the units, arrived. He told the officers what happened. Then the other officer heard the other driver's story. When the captain heard the other side, he flipped out. The captain started stomping around the street, cursing and yelling. We actually had to put him in the back of a cruiser to calm down. Now, if someone had a video camera and shot that footage, it would have been bad news for my agency. Furthermore, anytime he spoke he would use the wrong subject/verb agreement. Also, he would use words incorrectly. He was what we would call a typical nigga (TN).

My lieutenant was a black bitch; she was what we would call a chicken noodle on rye—a soup sandwich. The fact that I had a degree and she didn't made her have some animosity towards me, according to many people who knew her. Also, when they proposed the twenty-five day suspension, she told people in the community that I was going to serve twenty-five days. The reason this information got back to me was that many of the citizens had my phone number. They called me and advised of the things she said. When I didn't serve the days, I know she was looking stupid. I recall after all the grief she had caused me when my attorney had called the agency, this lieutenant wanted to act like she was my friend. I'm like, *Are you serious?* This lieutenant tried to burn me several times just because she was tired of answering the commander about my complaints. By the way, my complaints were never founded. This means there was no misconduct involved.

My sergeant, a black male, was great. He had been with the department since before I was born. If you didn't get along with this sergeant, then there was a problem with you. Even though he couldn't write and would ask me to help with writing his reports sometimes, I didn't mind. You know why? He was a great guy and funny as hell. This guy would never try to hurt anyone as a sergeant. Another sergeant, a black male who we used to call "Shitty Pants" because of the way he wore his pants to work, was an official who didn't do anything at his last district and was promoted. He was not exactly the most professional of people. He was lazy and didn't care. I would say he was in touch with his feminine side. For example, the area I worked in was a high crime area. I was responsible for a certain sector. There had been no violent crimes or any thefts from autos in my sector while I was on patrol. Then there was a call for a theft from auto in my sector. Of course I got a phone call from this sergeant asking me, "Why is there a theft from auto on your beat?" My response was, "Because I'm the only one down here. Perhaps if you put another unit down here, I would have some help." Furthermore, this was the first incident of a theft from auto in three months.

At my second district, I must say the officials were somewhat better but not a lot better. The commander, a white male, was okay, except when it came to training. He hated to see his officers trained. Any time I would put in for a training request he would deny it. The reasons he would deny the training were ridiculous. We had a general order in reference to training. Do you think management would abide by the general order? Hell no. Therefore, it was up to me to figure ways around the commander to get my training. When I did request training, I would have to speak to someone at the Police Academy before I would submit the training. All the academy would have to do was recommend approval; it didn't matter what the commander said. When the commander got word I was doing this he was furious. I would have to backdoor this guy just to get training.

For example, I wanted to go for training and he denied the paperwork. He then sent the paperwork to the academy. Little did he know, I had spoken to the person in charge of training, and he approved it. Then it was submitted to the commander of the academy for approval. It was approved. One thing a commander doesn't like is to have what he says overridden. So when I would see him, I would walk over to him and smile and shake his hand. I would say, "Hi, Commander, how are you?" Then he would ask my name. I would say, "I'm Officer Mac." He looked like he was about to kill me. Then I would laugh.

Another time, I requested training, but in a leave without pay status (LWOP); he denied it. Furthermore, he called human resources and spoke to the director and told her to deny me the training. I was calling human resources to find out the results. When I was told I was denied leave without pay, I was like, *How does someone deny you leave with out pay?* I just used my annual leave for the training. Now there was nothing they could do. But the next time he saw me he came over to me and shook my hand and asked how I was doing. I smiled at him and said, "Fine, how are you?" The look on his face was saying, *Fuck you*. There was a time I submitted a leave without pay request and he approved it. He didn't know what it was for. I used it for training. I remember word got back to him saying I used the leave for training. When he saw me on a barricaded suspect, he looked at me like, You *mother fucker*. I just smiled and said, "Hi Commander," and asked how his day was going.

Now what I don't understand is why you wouldn't want a better-trained officer. You know what a better-trained officer can do? Leave the department and obtain a better job. That's the reason they don't want you to train. It's like in slavery days, remember how they wouldn't teach the slave to read or write? That's because they didn't want the slave to have knowledge. The more knowledge you have, the more dangerous you become. It's almost like this: if they don't have it then they don't want you to have it. Guess what? I got mine. A good source of mine told me the commander knew I was trying to leave the department. Therefore, he was going to make it difficult for me to do so. What's the saying? Misery loves company. Without my training, I would still be there at that agency.

The inspectors: I had two or three good inspectors, one black male, one white male, and a black female. The female was a waste. The white one would be on patrol and answer some radio runs. He would also make traffic stops. If any officer was on a stop he would back you up. The best part about it was he wouldn't say anything to you on the stops. He would ask if you're okay and he would go somewhere else. He would never say anything to you on your scene. The scene was yours. The black one was good too. I don't think he cared anyway, which made things cool. He would come into roll call and smoke and joke with us. He also would be out on the street. He really didn't bother you. He would get in that ass if you messed up. Other than that, I can't say anything bad about this guy. Now, the female inspector I discussed in *Bitches in Law Enforcement*. Most of these women think they have something to prove. But this one, I don't know what her problem was. Maybe it's because she was a woman.

The captains: I had a black and white captain. The black captain was okay. He would never deny my training requests. All he had to do was approve or disapprove of the training. He would always say, "Mac, get that knowledge." But there were other times when he would just be a dick. I would just stay out of his way. For example, he would come into roll call and tell us to train like we fight. Now he was talking about an active shooter exercise we conducted. It was a total debacle. So me being an active shooter instructor, he made the comments while I was in roll call. I told him, "You don't train us, so how do you expect us to fight the way we train? You are leading the lambs to the slaughter." He said to me, "You're an active shooter instructor; why don't you train these guys?" I told him, "That's not my job. If you want me to train them, then send me to the academy." He got all flustered and just left the roll call room. Everyone in roll call was like, *You're telling him right*.

The white captain: I can't say anything bad about this guy. He's an all around great guy. If you did something wrong, then he would hammer you. But I really don't think he gave a fuck. That's what made him great. He would never fuck with the officers or come into roll call and say some dumb shit like the black captain did. This guy gets all the respect.

Lieutenants: I had two black males, two white males and a black female. Let's discuss the two black males. The one black male was an educated guy; he and I got along fine. I remember when I went for training, he told me to keep up the good work. He also told me, whatever it was I was doing, to keep it up. He loved to see knowledgeable officers. Anything he wanted done I would do for him. You know why? He was a good guy. The second black lieutenant was okay. He was more worried about the complaints I received and how to deal with them. I'm sure he was tired of writing and ending up with exonerated, or unfounded. When you become a pain in the ass to the officials, they will find a place for you. But overall, he wasn't too bad. Although, he loved to make a big production about nothing. The black female lieutenant was outstanding. She was my favorite out of all the black female officials I had. She was a great supervisor. She didn't micro-manage and she was about burning officers. Not only that, she was tired of the agency and all the bullshit they do. I was sorry to see her leave. She was truly a great supervisor and a great person.

The white lieutenants: the first one was good. He really didn't give a shit. That was the good thing. That meant he wasn't going to fuck with you. Just as long as you didn't get complaints, he didn't care. That meant I could do whatever I wanted. The second one was okay sometimes. The thing about this guy was he was a prick. The good thing about this guy—he was a prick to all of the officers. He showed no preferential treatment to any officer. I respected him for that. He was consistent as a supervisor. Many didn't like his ways, but he didn't bother me. So I had no problems with him.

Sergeants: two white males, two black females, and one black male. Let's start with the white sergeants. The first white sergeant was really good. He didn't micro-manage. He would ask you to do your job, but if you didn't, he really didn't care. He was laid-back and didn't want any problems from any of the officers. I can say this: he would back you up if need be. The second white sergeant actually became my lieutenant. This was the same guy I said was a prick. You have already read about him. The two black female sergeants, one of whom I almost wrote an entire chapter about, showed her lack of reasoning skills and how she was just a bitch. The second black female sergeant was outstanding. She was a great supervisor. She looked out for her people. Anything we could do for this supervisor, we would. We thought she was the greatest. This woman would stand up for the officers and we would stand up for her. She didn't micro-manage. If there was a problem, then she would try to resolve the issue. My first sergeant was a black male. He was actually pretty good. All he wanted people to do was to do their job. He really didn't try to burn anyone. If there was a problem he would handle it. If you as an officer needed anything, he would do his best to help you.

People must remember that bad supervision and doing things to people just because they can is wrong. Don't forget that we have problems as well. Sometimes that stress level can be too much to handle. People under stress can act in an abnormal fashion. Violence is a prime example. I'm shocked there has not been an active shooter situation at my agency because of the things the agency does for no reason. I made sure I was friends with the crazy officers—the ones who have the propensity to kill—so on the day the agency really pissed them off because they have other stressful things going on in their life, if they came to work shooting, they wouldn't shoot me. Trust me, everyone has his or her breaking point. Many times the agency does things just to make your life miserable. Sometimes we would joke about an active shooter situation with the officers in the locker room or in roll call. But everyone knows there is a little bit of truth in all jokes. Could you imagine if an officer came in to shoot up the police department because of a serious miscarriage of justice on the part of the agency, or the agency just fucking with an officer because they could? This happens all the time. I'll bet your policy changes would be made effective. Outside agencies would be called in to investigate my agency.

In closing, you will see I have had good supervisors, mediocre supervisors, and piss poor supervisors. It's funny, if you talk to cops, the things they say about supervisors are negative. Once again, I weigh the good against the bad. It seems the bad outweighs the good.

Chapter Ten

Professionalism or a Lack Thereof

As a police officer working for a major police department there are certain standards that should be maintained. For example, males should have their hair neatly trimmed, cut close, or bald. No dreadlocks, braids, twists, or platts should be worn. The reason for this is because, as a police officer, you must look like a respectable individual. One should not look like the ones we arrest. I can understand undercover work; that makes sense. But as a patrol officer, that is unacceptable. This is supposed to be a paramilitary environment. In reality, this agency is ghetto as hell. As I said, this agency has low standards. Matter of fact, it has no standards.

For example, I was told by my background investigator that I was not supposed to be hired because the agency felt I was too educated. In fact, they were going to hire another individual who had a criminal record, but the individual was a relative of a member of the department. Now keep in mind, I had six years of prior law enforcement experience, a former police misconduct investigator from another agency and a bachelors degree. This will show you the lack of professionalism or the low standards this agency has. As I stated in: *Bitches in Law Enforcement*, these black bitches like drug dealers as boyfriends. I want to know who is conducting the vetting process for these women. There is no way the majority of these black women should get hired. I think they have to be doing some favors for the background investigators.

Now, when I went for the preliminary test and the background, I was shocked. I saw a white male with tattoos on his arms and with a ponytail. I was thinking, *This guy must be an undercover or worked vice.* I then spoke up about this white male. Then someone said, "He's a patrol officer." I was like, "Oh, hell naw." I knew I was in for some problems.

Now, when I was in the academy, there was a recruit officer arrested for selling guns. Guess what? His father was a detective on the department. I'm thinking to myself, *Should I leave this place now?* Even when I arrived at my first district, I was always clean-shaven, uniform pressed, shoes and brass polished. Don't you know, I was ridiculed for looking professional. But, I was working in the hood. During roll call, a comment was made when I was training a new officer. A veteran officer said, "Frank, why does your training officer (TO) look better than you?" I was the TO. Now many officers, especially veteran officers, don't care about how they look. Then, I couldn't understand, but now I have a better understanding. For example, there was an officer who would come to work with long hair, a beard, and his uniform didn't fit him very well. We used to call him Serpico. It was only until a sergeant spoke to another official and that official told Serpico to get his hair and beard cut or face discipline. The next day, this officer was a changed individual. No beard, no long hair. He is now up to department specifications. Furthermore, Serpico was a new officer.

We also had an official on the department who had twists with shells on the ends of his hair. I was like, *Are you serious? What the fuck is going on here?* Keep in mind, I have not seen any officials from any other agencies with hair like that. This is professionalism.

I remember during Thanksgiving, many of the officers had to work. One official (Stuttering Stanley, we'll discuss him later) told us we had to pay to eat. This made sense, but when he said it was going to be ghetto fabulous up in this mutha fucker. I said, "This ghettoass sergeant." This is typical for this agency. They embrace ignorance and ghetto people. That's what the DMV is made up of.

As I have resigned from this agency, this is what occurred. I was told they were not allowing me to resign. Matter of fact, the agency said they were not accepting my resignation. Furthermore, the agency said I didn't give them a 30-day notice to leave the job. I told them this was only a courtesy; I didn't have to tell them. I could just leave. An official said, "Well, you're in violation." I started to laugh and said, "Okay, I'll tell you what, I'll leave my belongings in a box and you can come pick them up at my residence." Then they threatened to fine me $5,000 dollars if I left. Then they said, "You will be marked AWOL (absent without leave) if you are not at work on a certain day. I started laughing. I asked, "How are you going to mark me AWOL if I quit?" What the Fuck?

The next day, I was given a clearance form from a source of mine to check out. I had to go to certain divisions and have the divisions sign stating I didn't own anything. When it was time for the exit interview, I went to the Human Resources Department (HR). When I asked to speak with someone for the interview, a sergeant came out and told me he was not going to accept the form. I told him, "Okay," and left the form on the counter with "refused to give exit interview" marked on it. Then I asked the administrative assistant to make me copies of the paperwork. The sergeant told me my chain of command failed to submit the paperwork in a timely manner. I told him, "That's not my problem, that's your problem" He said, "No, it's your problem, and you have to deal with it." The problem is I have paperwork showing I have abided by the clearing procedures. My last word to the sergeant was, "Bye."

The day prior, I was at Human Resources and spoke with a lieutenant and asked for the clearance form. He told me he wasn't permitted to give me the form because the chief had not accepted my resignation. I asked him if there was anywhere to obtain this form. He stated, "You can only get the form here," with his smug attitude. Little did he know, I already had the form. I was playing stupid with him, letting him think I was stuck. I was just fucking with him. Can you believe an agency not allowing an individual to resign? What a fucking joke.

Here are some more examples of the same. There was a retired police officer from New York City who worked for my agency. He told them he quit. He also was told he was not able to quit without a 30-day notice. His response was, "Notice I won't be here for the next 30 days and fuck you." He also made it clear that this was the worst agency to work for.

This great agency of mine was investigating an officer for excessive force. Of course, they were going to stick it to him. Thank God for an independent investigator who had proof that this officer was not involved. This officer wasn't putting up with any more of my agency's bullshit, so he left. No resignation, nothing. Eventually, one of the supervisors called this officer and asked if he was coming to work after a two-week period. The officer said, "I quit." The sergeant said "You have to turn in your uniforms and equipment." The officer replied, "That shit is in my locker." The sergeant asked what the combination to the locker was. The officer said, "Ask the administrative person." Apparently, one time an official gave this officer a blueprint of a certain location. Now, this officer had this blueprint and the official needed it back. The official called the officer and said, "I need the document." The officer responded, "I wiped my ass with it." The official said, "Send it or I'll get a warrant for your arrest for theft." The officer said, "Go ahead, I don't even live in the surrounding area. The warrant will be non-extraditable, so FUCK YOU."

If you think the first three are outlandish, wait until you read this one. There was an officer who left my agency and went to another agency. He just quit. He said the agency was ridiculous and quit. Apparently, he didn't conduct the clearing procedures correctly. So my agency applied for a warrant for his arrest for some property that was missing. The best part about this is the judge signed off on the warrant. Of course, the warrant was non-extraditable but this just goes to show you how fucked up this agency could be. Then they wonder why they can't keep people.

There was a sergeant in my district; we used to call him Stuttering Stanley. We wouldn't have fucked with him, but he was a prick. Now he's a big guy, but not too bright. Well, officials like that are targets for a police officer's wrath. This sergeant would come over the air and ask for our statistics. This is what a transmission would sound like:

> *Stuttering Stanley: All units switch to the TAC channel for your stats.*
> *So we'd switch to the TAC channel.*
> *One unit would come over the air: Five movers, two parkers.*
> *Another unit: One mover, three parkers.*
> *Another unit: Seven movers, five parkers.*
> *Mac: Zero.*

Stuttering Stanley: Zero.
Mac: Yeah, zero as in zero.
Stuttering Stanley: Mac, why do you have zero stats? Be advised you are speaking with an official.
Mac: Be advised I know you're an official and I still have zero stats. By the way, I just got to work.
Stuttering Stanley: C-c-c-call me in the s-s-s-s-sergeants office.
Mac: C-c-c-c-copy.

There was another incident with Stuttering Stanley. We were called for stats and I told him I had a certain number of stats for a certain category. When it was time for check-off, another official told me that Stanley wanted to see me. According to the other official, Stanley was attempting to get me for lying on the air. I walked up to the sergeant's office and asked if he wanted to see me. I was told to "stand by" while he looked up the transmissions on the computer and what was said. When he saw I didn't say what he thought I said, he became furious, clinched his hands, and yelled, "LEAVE!" I asked, "Is everything okay?" and then smiled at him. I then said, "Have a good night, Sergeant."

As you can see, if you want to fuck with me, I'm going to fuck with you. You can imagine, ever since that incident, he was out to get me. But when you as an official get pissed off and want to get back at an officer, this can turn into harassment. Not only that, there is no legitimate reason to do what you are doing. It's just your egos bruised. That's because your emotions are involved.

An officer will always win in the long-term if he documents what he believes to be the alleged misconduct. The officer should file a complaint against that official. Then that complaint will stay in that official's jacket for a certain period of time.

Here is another example, I asked for outside training and was told the training didn't apply to my position. Although, active shooter applies to patrol officers. The best part about the training was that it was free. All I had to do was pay for my travel, lodging, and food. I sought out assistance from a sergeant who had knowledge of active shooter. Now, this sergeant told me to bring him the paperwork and he would talk to my commander for me. Once he found out I was denied administrative leave, he placed a call to the agency conducting the training. He told them, "Mac won't be attending training; I'm going to take his place." When I went to work the next day, he called the district, and said, "Mac, since you won't be going to this training, I'm going to take your spot." I told him I was going to the training. He responded, "How? You were denied administrative leave." I told him I was taking annual leave. He was like, "Oh." When I arrived at the location of the training one of the instructors asked me, "What is up with your agency? Is that the way your agency conducts business?" It was pretty bad because it was the director of the training facility who told the instructor to see how I was doing. The director even came up to me and said, "Your supervisor tried to fuck you out of this position." I was like, *Pretty much*. The director said, "That's not good."

Now what type of message does this send to other departments, because they will talk to one another? What does this director of training think of my agency? I'm sure he thinks it's a professional agency. Furthermore, he was an official from a different law enforcement agency. This action the sergeant did is just business as usual from my agency. I know what you are thinking; *This is a professional agency.*

There have been officers who have married or even just had relationships. Many times these officers have had domestic violence issues like shooting at each other. Many an officer has been struck by another officer's bullet. This is common in my agency. This has happened multiple times.

Other things happen, such as sexual harassment or even sexual assault. There was a captain at my first district who was transferred because he was not able to keep his hands to himself. Of course, nothing happens to management on this job. If this were an officer, he would have received a suspension. There was a sergeant accused of harassing a white female. Of course the department backed the white officer's story and demoted the black sergeant. That sergeant is now an officer. There was an officer I worked with who was accused of licking a female officer on her face and grabbing her ass. They transferred the officer and he did something similar again at the district he was transferred to. The department eventually fired him.

There was a lieutenant who was charged with second-degree sexual assault. The story is allegedly that he grabbed a female sergeant and made her sit on his lap. According to the female sergeant, the lieutenant's dick was hard when she fell on his lap. Bottom line, when it went to court, they dropped the sexual charge and gave him a simple assault. But he can keep his job. This lieutenant was a good guy; he was from the same area as me. Matter of fact, he was a funny guy. As you can see, he wasn't the most professional.

This is a sad incident: Two black bitches were at court in uniform and were involved first in a verbal altercation, and then a physical altercation about another male officer who was married. What the fuck? The cackling hens are at it again. Listen, it doesn't get anymore unprofessional than that. C'mon now, in uniform and fighting over a married man? Both females kept their jobs. That is some ghetto shit fo sho. But as I said, this is normal for this agency. The funny thing is it is accepted. This agency pays out more money for lawsuits because of the foolishness the officials and officers do. There was an official who placed a suspect in the trunk of his police cruiser. Of course this official is a high-ranking member of the department. There are so many officials and officers who have Police Department Identification Numbers (PDID) numbers. I'm starting to think maybe there is something wrong with me.

In early 2002, there was an IMF World Bank Protest. During the protest, many of the protestors were arrested without warning allegedly. Of course they filed suit and won. Now, the thing about this is when it came time for the videotapes of the arrests and the radio transmissions, they were altered. A criminal probe was launched into this and the happenings. Many high-ranking officials were brought in front of a US District Magistrate. This Magistrate informed these Command officials of their fifth amendments rights.

The last one really shows how this agency works. This was in the paper as well. Recently, an assistant chief was placed on administrative leave for giving command staff members answers to an open book exam. I know many of you are asking, *How does one gives answers to an open book exam?* If you have a deadline and can't or won't meet the deadline, you might need some help. Also, if you're not interested in the material, you might not give a shit and ask for assistance. Now, as a supervisor you have to monitor your people and ask them whether they're close to finishing the exam. If not, they may need some help. According to sources, this test had to do with criminal intelligence (CRIMINT). This is not dealing with how smart or dumb a criminal is, but systems of tracking people, patterns of criminals, and handling confidential sources. I was informed this was the same test given to agents from the Federal Bureau of Investigation. According to sources within the department, this assistant chief emailed the answers out to members of her command staff, so they could complete their exams in time. This was an integrity violation; it was cheating. The best part about this is she admitted to the wrongdoing.

Do you know how many officers who have been caught cheating at the academy lost their jobs? Now what about the command staff that accepted the answers? Are they just as guilty? When the assistant chief was placed on leave, the news had to have been on every news station in the DMV. Every newspaper had an article about it. Now when she was put back to work, there may have been some discipline issued; maybe there wasn't. The bottom line is, as a police officer, regardless of your rank, you are held to a higher standard. What kind of message does that send to the other officers? Is this a message of, *It's okay to cheat*? If so, then all of the officers who were caught cheating at the academy on tests should be reinstated. You can't have a double standard.

This is how this agency works; there is a lack of professionalism within the ranks. If I had cheated on an exam or given answers, there would be no questions asked, and termination papers would have been written up. I would have been given a trial board and been terminated just like that. Around this agency, the words *honor* and *integrity* have no meaning. They are just words. It's a shame to have been taught a code of ethics in the academy, when the ethical standards don't apply. Well, let me say this much: ethics apply to people they want to apply them to. But once again, this is Washington, DC and this is business as usual.

Conclusion

This it what it's like to be a cop in a police department; well, at least this agency. People don't understand why cops don't smile and don't like to be bothered. We deal with everything in society. The average person can't relate to a police officer. We have two different perspectives on what's going on in the world. Many people would say I'm a racist, bigot, homophobe, or a male chauvinist. The fact is I'm not. If I am those things, society and my experiences have made me this way. This is, of course, based upon my experiences and dealing with citizens. This job will change you. If you were Mr. Nice guy before you took this job, you won't be for long. It would be different if I hadn't dealt with all these different groups of people and I had these views. I have justified my views because of my dealing with you all. I know you might think cops are crazy, but the truth is I respond to your craziness. You're the ones who call for help. Cops don't call you, you call us. After a while, citizens start to be a pain in the ass.

There is not one group better than the other. Blacks aren't better than whites. Whites aren't better than blacks. The black sophisticated educated bitch is no better than the common woman. I'll say this, blacks are better than niggaz; believe that. However, they are equally fucked up. The groups are just fucked up in different ways, as I have written in the book.

As you can see, I'm not politically correct. The best part about it is, I don't give a shit. This is how cops talk among each other. Most police officers will deny this, but we do. We would never use this type of language in public, but when we are alone, we're just like you citizens. I'll bet you citizens use the same words when referring to gender, races, and sexual orientation. Many of you say you don't; I beg to differ. Matter of fact, my views are conservative. I'm sure people are thinking, *He's a Republican*. Guess what? I'm not a Republican or a Democrat. To me they are one in the same. All I know is I'm conservative in my views. If you had liberal views before you started this job, I'm sure they would change over time.

As I said in the introduction, I have to maintain a certain mindset to function in this kind of environment. It's to keep me sharp and to make me realize what I do for a profession. Now you have seen a portion of my world. It's lovely.